Grant Allen, Peter M

Babylon

Volume 3

Grant Allen, Peter Macnab

Babylon
Volume 3

ISBN/EAN: 9783337503048

Printed in Europe, USA, Canada, Australia, Japan

Cover: Foto ©ninafisch / pixelio.de

More available books at **www.hansebooks.com**

BABYLON

By Grant Allen

(Cecil Power)

Author Of 'Philistia' 'Strange Stories' Etc.

In Three Volumes

Vol. III.

With Twelve Illustrations By P. Macnab

London

Chatto & Windus, Piccadilly
1885

'So this was Cæoi!'

Original

B A B Y L O N

BY

GRANT ALLEN

(CECIL POWER)

AUTHOR OF 'PHILISTIA' 'STRANGE STORIES' ETC.

IN THREE VOLUMES

VOL. III.

WITH TWELVE ILLUSTRATIONS BY P. MACNAB

London

CHATTO & WINDUS, PICCADILLY

1885

[The right of translation is reserved]

Original

CONTENTS

CHAPTER XXIX. A VIEW OF ROME, By Hiram Winthrop.

In the midst of an undulating sunlit plain, fresh with flowers in spring, burnt and yellow in summer and autumn, a great sordid shrivelled city blinks and festers visibly among the rags and tatters in the eye of day. Within its huge imperial walls the shrunken modern town has left a broad skirt of unoccupied hillocks; low mounds covered by stunted straggling vineyards, or broken here and there by shabby unpicturesque monasteries, with long straight pollard-lined roads stretching interminably in dreary lines between the distant boundaries. In the very centre, along some low flats that bound a dull, muddy, silent river, the actual inhabited city itself crouches humbly beneath the mouldering ruins of a nobler age. A shapeless mass of dingy, weather-stained, discoloured, tile-roofed buildings, with all its stucco peeling in the sun, it lies crowded and jammed into a narrow labyrinth of tortuous alleys, reeking with dirt, and rich in ragged filthy beggars. One huge lazaretto of sin and pestilence, choked with the accumulated rubbish and kitchen-middens of forty centuries—that was Hiram Winthrop's Rome—the Rome which fate and duty compelled him to exchange for the wild woods and the free life of untrammelled nature.

Step into one of the tortuous alleys, and you see this abomination of desolation even more distinctly, under the pitiless all-exposing glare of an Italian sky. The blotchy walls rise so high into the air to right and left, that they make the narrow lane gloomy even at midday; and yet, the light pours down obliquely upon the decaying plaster with so fierce a power that every rent and gap and dirt-stain stands out distinctly, crying in vain to the squalid tenants in the dens within to repair its unutterable dilapidation. Beneath, the little slippery pavement consists of herringbone courses of sharp stones; overhead, from ropes fastened across the street, lines of rags and tatters flutter idly in the wind, proving (what Hiram was otherwise inclined to doubt) that people at Rome *do* sometimes ostensibly wash their garments, or at least damp them. Dark gloomy shops line either side; shops windowless and doorless, entered and closed by shutters, and just rendered visible by the feeble lamp that serves a double duty as lightener of the general darkness, and taper to the tiny painted shrine of the wooden Madonna. A world of hungry ragged men, hungry dirty slatternly women, hungry children playing in the gutter, hungry priests pervading the very atmosphere—that on a closer view was Rome as it appeared to Hiram Winthrop.

To be sure, there was a little more of it. Up towards the Corso and Piazza del Popolo, there was a gaunt, modern Haussmannised quarter, the Rome of the strangers—cleaner by a fraction, whiter by a great deal, less odorous by a trifle, but still to Hiram Winthrop utterly flat, stale, and unprofitable. The one Rome was ugly, if picturesque; the other Rome was modern, and not even ugly.

Work at Seguin's studio was also to Hiram a wretched mockery of an artistic training. The more he saw of the French painter, the more he disliked him: and what was worse, the dislike was plainly mutual. For Audouin's sake, because Audouin had wished it, Hiram went on working feebly at historical pictures which he hated and could never possibly care for; but he panted to be free from the wretched bondage at once and for ever. Two years after his arrival in Rome, where he was now living upon the little capital he had derived from the sale of the deacon's farm, Hiram determined, on Audouin's strenuous advice, by letter delivered, to send a tentative painting to Paris for the Salon. Seguin watched it once or twice in the course of its completion, but he only shrugged his lean shoulders ominously, and muttered incomprehensible military oaths to himself, which he had picked up half a century before from his father, the ex-corporal. (On the strength of that early connection with the army, Seguin, in spite of his shrivelled frame, still affected a certain swaggering military air and bearing upon many occasions.) When it was finished, he looked at it a trifle contemptuously, and then murmured: 'Good. That will finish him. After that——-' An ugly grimace did duty for the rest of the sentence.

Still, Hiram sent it in, as Audouin had desired of him; and in due time received the formal intimation from the constituted authorities of the Salon that his picture had been rejected. He knew it would be, and yet he felt the disappointment bitterly. Sitting alone in his room that evening (for he would not let even Colin share his sorrow) he brooded gloomily by himself, and began to reflect seriously that after all his whole life had been one long and wretched failure. There was no denying it, he had made a common but a fatal error; he had mistaken the desire to paint for the power of painting. He saw it all quite clearly now, and from that moment his whole career seemed in his eyes to be utterly dwarfed and spoiled and blighted.

There was only one part of each of those four years of misery at Rome that Hiram could ever afterwards look back upon with real pleasure. Once every summer, he and Colin started off together for a month's relaxation in the Tyrol or Switzerland. On those trips, Hiram forgot all the rest of his life altogether, and lived for thirty clear days in a primitive paradise. His sketch-book went always with him, and he even ventured to try his hand upon a landscape or two in oils, now that he was well out of the way of Seguin's chilly magisterial interference. Colin Churchill always praised them warmly: 'But then Colin, you know' (Hiram said to himself). 'is always such a generous enthusiastic fellow. He has such a keen artistic eye himself, of course, that he positively reads beauty into the weakest efforts of any other beginner. Still, I do feel that I can put my soul into drawing these rocks and mountains, which I never can do in painting a dressed-up model in an artificial posture, and pretending that I think she's really Cleopatra. If one had the genuine Cleopatra to paint, now, exactly as she threw herself naturally down upon her own Egyptian sofa, why that might possibly be quite another matter. But, even so, Cleopatra could never have moved me half so much as the gloss on the chestnuts and the shimmer of the cloud-light on the beautiful purple water down below there.'

Sometimes, too, Hiram took Colin with him out into the Campagna; not that he loved the Campagna—there was an odour of Rome about it; but still at least it was a sort of country, and to Hiram Winthrop that was everything. One day, in his fourth year in Italy, he was sitting on a spring afternoon with Colin beside the arches of a broken aqueduct in that great moorland, which he had been using as the foreground for a little water-colour. He had finished his sketch, and was holding it at different angles before him, when Colin suddenly broke the silence by saying warmly: 'Some day, Winthrop, I'm sure you must sell them.'

Hiram shook his head despondently. 'No, no, Churchill,' he answered with a half-angry wave of his disengaged hand. 'Even while I was at Seguin's, I knew I could never do anything worth looking at, and since I took this little studio myself, I feel sure of it. It's only your kindness that makes you think otherwise.'

Colin took the sketch from him for a moment and eyed it carefully. 'My dear fellow,' he said at last, 'believe me, you're mistaken. Just look at that! Why, Winthrop, I tell you candidly, I'm certain there's genius in it.'

Hiram smiled bitterly. 'No, no, not genius, I assure you,' he answered with a sigh, 'but only the longing for it. You have genius, I have nothing more than aspiration.'

Yet in his own heart, when Colin once more declared he was mistaken, Hiram Winthrop, looking at that delicate sketch, did almost for the moment pluck up courage again, and agree with his friend that if only the public would but smile upon him, he, too, might really do something worth the looking at.

He went home, indeed, almost elated, after so many months of silent dejection, by that new-born hope. When he reached their rooms in the alley (for Colin, in his desire to save, still stood by him, in spite of altered fortunes) he found a large official envelope of French pattern lying casually upon the table. He knew it at once; it bore the official seal of the Académie Française. He tore open the letter hastily. Was it possible that this time they might really have hung him? What did it say? Let him see... A stereotyped form.... 'Regret to announce to you.... great claims upon their attention.... compelled to refuse admission to the painting submitted to their consideration by M. Winthrop.'

Hiram let the letter drop out of his hands without a word. For the third time, then, his picture had been rejected for the Paris Salon!

A day or iwo later, the agent to whom he always confided his works for the necessary arrangements, wrote to him with florid French politeness on the subject of its final disposal. Last year he had been able to give Monsieur but forty francs for his picture, while the year before he had felt himself justified in paying sixty. Unfortunately, neither of these pictures had yet been sold; Monsieur's touch evidently

12

did not satisfy the exacting Parisian public. This year, he regretted to tell Monsieur, he would be unable to offer him anything for the picture itself; but he would take back the frame at an inestimable depreciation on the original figure. He trusted to merit Monsieur's honoured commands upon future occasions.

Those four pounds were all the money Hiram had yet earned, in four years, by the practice of his profession; and the remains of the deacon's patrimony would hardly now suffice to carry him through another winter.

But then, that winter, Gwen was coming.

If it had not been for the remote hope of still seeing Gwen before he left Rome for ever, Hiram was inclined to think the only bed he would have slept in, that dreary, weary, disappointing night, was the bed of the Tiber.

CHAPTER XXX. MINNA'S RESOLUTION.

As Minna Wroe opened her eyes that morning in the furnished house in the Via Clementina, she could hardly realise even now that she was actually at Rome, and within half-an-hour's walk of dear Colin.

Yes, that was mainly how the Eternal City, the capital of art, the centre of Christendom, the great museum of all the ages, envisaged itself as of course to the frank barbarism of poor wee Minna's simple little bosom. Some of us, when we go to Rome, see in it chiefly a vast historical memory—the Forum, the Colosseum, the arch of Titus, the ruined Thermæ, the Palace of the Caesars. Some of us see in it rather a magnificent panorama of ancient and modern art, the Vatican, St. Peter's, the Apollo, the Aphrodite, the great works of Michael Angelo, and Raphael, and the spacious broad-souled Renaissance painters. Some see in it a modern gimcrack Italian metropolis; some, a fashionable English winter residence; some, a picturesque, quaint old-world mediæval city; some, a Babylon doomed before long to a terrible fiery destruction; and some, a spiritual centre of marvellous activity, with branches that ramify out in a thousand directions over the entire civilised and barbarous world. But Minna Wroe thought of that wonderful composite heterogeneous Rome for the most part merely as the present home and actual arena of Colin Churchill, sculptor, at Number 84 in the Via Colonna.

It had been a grand piece of luck for Minna, the chance that brought her the opportunity of taking that long-looked-for, and much desired journey. To be sure, she had been very happy in her own way down in the pretty little rural Surrey village. Mr. O'Donovan was the kindest and most fatherly old clergyman that ever lived; and though he *did* bother her just a little now and then with teaching in the Sunday school and conducting the Dorcas society, and taking charge of the Mothers' meeting, still he was so good and gentle and sympathetic to her at all times, that Minna could easily have forgiven him for twice as much professional zeal as he ever himself displayed in actual reality. Yet for all that, though the place was so pretty, and the work so light, and the four little girls on the whole such nice pleasant well-behaved little mortals, Minna certainly did miss Colin very terribly. Some employers would doubtless have said to themselves when they saw the governess moping and melancholy in spite of all the comfort that was provided for her: 'Well, what more on earth that girl can possibly be wanting really passes my poor finite comprehension.' But Mr. O'Donovan knew better. He was one of those people who habitually and instinctively put themselves in the place of others; and when on Sunday mornings after the letter with the twenty-five centesimi stamp had arrived at the rectory, he saw poor Minna moving about the house before church, looking just a trifle tearful, he said to himself with a shake of his dear kindly old broken-nosed head: 'Ah well, ah well; young people will be young people; and I've often noticed that however comfortable a girl of twenty-two may be in all externals, why, God bless my soul, if she's got a lover five hundred miles away, she can't help crying a bit about him every now and then—and very natural!' Minna gratefully observed too, that on all such occasions Mr. O'Donovan treated her with more than his usual consideration, and seemed to understand exactly what it was that made her rather sharper than her wont with the small feelings of the four little ones.

And Mr. O'Donovan never forgot his promise to Minna to

look out for a family who were going to Rome and who wanted an English governess. 'But, bless my soul,' he thought to himself, 'who on earth would ever have believed beforehand what a precious difficult thing it is to find a person who fulfils at once both the conditions? People going to Rome, dozens of 'em; people wanting a governess, dozens of 'em also; but people going to Rome *and* wanting a governess, I regret to say, not a soul to be heard of. Sounds just like a Senate House problem, when I was a young fellow at Cambridge: If out of x A's there are y B's and z C's, what are the chances that any B is also a C?

Answer, precious little.' Indeed, the good old parson even went the length of putting an advertisement into the *Guardian* twice a year, without saying a word about it to Minna: 'A Clergyman (beneficed) wishes to recommend highly qualified Young Lady as English nursery Governess to a Family wintering at Rome.' But he never got a single answer. 'Dear, dear,' the kind old gentleman muttered to himself, on each such occasion when the post passed by day after day without bringing him a single one of the expected applications, 'that's always the way, unfortunately. Advertise that you want a governess, and you have fifty poor young girls answering at once, wasting a penny stamp a-piece, and waiting eagerly to know whether you'll be kindly pleased to engage 'em. Advertise that you want a place as governess, and never a soul will take a moment's notice of you. Supply and demand, I believe they call it in the newspapers; supply and demand; but in a Christian country one might have imagined they'd have got something more charitable to give us by this time than the bare gospel of Political Economy. When I was young, we didn't understand Political Economy; and Mr. Malthus, who wrote about it, used to be considered little better than a heathen. Still, I've done my duty, as far as I've been able; that's one comfort. And if I can't succeed in getting a place for George Wroe's daughter

16

to go and join this wonderful clever lover of hers at Rome (confound the fellow, he's making a pot of money I see by the papers; why the dickens doesn't he send over and fetch her?)—well anyhow, dear Lucy's children are getting the benefit of her attention, meanwhile, and what on earth I should do without her now, I'm sure I haven't the slightest conception.'

At last, however, after one of these regular six-monthly notices the rector happened to come down to breakfast one morning, and found a letter in a strange foreign-looking hand lying beside his porridge on the dining-room table. He turned it over and looked anxiously at the back:—yes, it was just as he hoped and feared; it bore a London post-mark, and had a Byzantine-look-ing coronet embossed upon it in profuse gilding and brilliantly blazoned heraldic colours. The old man's heart sank within him. 'Confound it,' he said to himself, half-angrily, 'I do believe I've gone and done my duty this time with a regular vengeance. This is an answer to the advertisement at last, and it's an application from somebody or other to carry off dear little Miss Wroe to Rome as somebody's governess. Hang it all, how shall I ever manage, at my age too, to accommodate myself to another young woman! I won't open it now. I can't open it now. If I open it before prayers and breakfast, and it really turns out to be quite satisfactory, I shall break down over it, I know I shall; and then little Miss Wroe will see I've been crying about it, and refuse to leave us—she's a good girl, and if she knew how much I valued her, she'd refuse to leave us; and so after all she'd never get to join this sculptor son of young Sam Churchill's that she's for ever thinking of. I'll put it away till after breakfast. Perhaps indeed it mayn't be at all the thing for her—which would be very lucky—no, I mean unlucky;—well, there, there, what a set of miserable selfish wretched creatures we are really, whenever it comes to making even a small sacrifice for one another. Con

17

O'Donovan, my boy, you know perfectly well in your heart of hearts you were half-wishing that that poor girl wasn't going at last to join her lover that she's so distracted about; and yet after that, you have the impudence to get up in the pulpit every Sunday morning, and preach a sermon about our duty to others to your poor parishioners—perhaps, even out of the fifth chapter of Matthew, you confounded hypocrite! It seems to me there's a good deal of truth in that line of Tennyson's, though it sounds so cynical:

However we brave it out, we men are a little breed!

Upon my soul, when I come to think of it, I'm really and truly quite ashamed of myself.'

Do you ever happen to have noticed that the very men who have the smallest possible leaven of littleness, or meanness, or selfishness, in their own natures are usually the exact ones who most often bitterly reproach themselves for their moral shortcomings in this matter?

When the rector came to open the envelope by-and-by in his own study, he found it contained a letter in French from a Russian countess, then in London, who proposed spending the winter in Italy. 'Madame had seen M. O'Donovan's Advertisement in a journal of his country, and would be glad to learn from Monsieur some particulars about the young lady whom he desired to recommend to families. Madame required a governess for one little girl, and proposed a salary of 2,500 francs.' The old man's eyes brightened at the idea of so large an offer—one hundred pounds sterling—and then he laid down the letter again, and cried gently to himself, as old people sometimes do, for a few minutes. After that, he reflected that Georgey Wroe's daughter was a very good girl, and deserved any advancement that he could get for her; and Georgey was a fine young fellow himself, and as clever a hand at managing a small smack in a squall off the Chesil as any fisherman, bar none, in all England. God bless his soul, what a run that was they had together, the night the 'Sunderbund' East Indiaman went to pieces off Deadman's Bay, from Seaton Bar right round the Bill to Lulworth! He could mind even now the way the water broke over the gunwale into Georgey's face, and how Georgey laughed at the wind, and swore it was a mere breeze, and positively whistled to it. Well, well, he would do what he could for Georgey's daughter, and he must look out (with a stifled sigh) for some other good girl to take care of Lucy's precious little ones.

So he sat down and wrote off such a glowing account of Minna's many virtues to the Russian countess in London— an account mainly derived from his own calm inner belief as to what a perfect woman's character ought to be made up of —that the Russian countess wrote back to say she would engage Mdlle. Wroe immediately, without even waiting to see her. Till he got that answer, Mr. O'Donovan never said a word about the matter to Minna, for fear she might be disappointed; but as soon as it arrived, and he had furtively dried his eyes behind his handkerchief, lest she should see how sorry he was to lose her, he laid the two letters triumphantly down before her, and said, in a voice which seemed as though he were quite as much interested in the event as she was: 'There you see, my dear, I've found somebody at last for you to go to Rome with.' Minna's head reeled and her eyes swam as she read the two letters to herself with some difficulty (for her French was of the strictly school-taught variety); but as soon as she had spelt out the meaning to her own intense satisfaction, she flung her arms round old Mr. O'Donovan's neck, and kissed him twice fervently. Mr. O'Donovan's eyes glistened, and he kissed her in return gently on her forehead. She had grown to be to him almost like a daughter, and he loved her so dearly that it was a hard wrench to part from her. 'And you know, my dear,' he said to her with fatherly tenderness, 'you won't mind my mentioning it to you, I'm sure, because I need hardly tell you how much interest I take in my old friend Georgey's daughter; but I think it's just as well the lady's a foreigner, and especially a Russian, because they're not so particular, I believe, about the conventionalities of society as our English mothers are apt to be; and you'll probably get more opportunities of seeing young Churchill when occasion offers than you would have done if you'd happened to have gone abroad with an English family.'

When Minna went away from the country rectory, at very short notice, some three weeks later, Mary the housemaid observed, with a little ill-natured smile to the other village gossips, that it wasn't before it was time, neither; for the way that that there Miss Wroe, as she called herself, had been carrying on last month or two along of poor old master, and him a clergyman, too, and old enough to know better, but there, what can you expect, for everybody knows what an old gentleman is when a governess or anybody can twist him round her little finger, was that dreadful that really she often wondered whether a respectable girl as was always brought up quite decent and her only a fisherman's daughter, too, as master hisself admitted, but them governesses, when they got theirselves a little eddication and took a sitooation, was that stuck-up and ridiculous, not but what *she* made her always keep her place, for that matter, for *she* wasn't going to be put down by none of your governesses, setting themselves up to be ladies when they wasn't no better nor she was, but at any rate it was a precious good thing she was gone now before things hadn't gone no further, for if she'd stayed, why, of course, there wouldn't have been nothing left for her to do, as had always lived in proper families, but to go and give notice herself afore she'd stop in such a sitooation.

And Mrs. Upjohn, the doctor's wife, smiled blandly when

Mary spoke to her about it, and said in a grave tone of severe moral censure: 'Well, there, Mary, you oughtn't to want to meddle with your master's business, whatever you may happen to fancy. Not but what Miss Wroe herself certainly did behave in a most imprudent and unladylike manner; and I can't deny, of course, that she's laid herself open to every word of what you say about her. But then, you know, Mary, she isn't a lady; and, after all, what can you expect from such a person?' To which Mary, having that profound instinctive contempt for her own class which is sometimes begotten among the essentially vulgar by close unconscious introspection, immediately answered: 'Ah, what indeed!' and went on unrebuked with her ill-natured gossip. So high and watchful is social morality amid the charming Arcadian simplicity of our outlying English country villages.

But poor little Minna, waking up that very morning in the Via Clementina, never heeded their venomous backbiting one bit, and thought only of going to see her dear Colin. What a surprise it would be to him to see her, to be sure; for Minna, fearful that the scheme might fall through before it was really settled, had written not a word to him about it beforehand, and meant to surprise him by dropping in upon him quite unexpectedly at his studio without a single note of warning.

'Ah, my dear,' the countess said to her, when Minna, trembling, asked leave to go out and visit her cousin—that dim relationship, so inevitable among country folk from the same district, had certainly more than once done her good service—'you have then a parent at Rome, a sculptor? Yes, yes, I recall it; that good Mr. O'Donovan made mention to me of this parent. He prayed me to let you have the opportunity from time to time of visiting him. These are our first days at Rome. For the moment, Olga will demand her vacations: she will wish to distract herself a little with the town, before she applies herself seriously to her studies of English. Let us say to-day, then: let us say this very morning. You can go, my child: you can visit your parent: and if his studio encloses anything of artistic, you pass me the word, I go to see it. But if they have the instinct of the family strong, these English! I find that charming; it is delicious: it is all that there is of most pure and poetical. She wishes to visit her cousin, who is a sculptor and whom she has not seen, it is now a long time; and she blushes and trembles like a French demoiselle who comes from departing the day itself from the gates of the convent. One would say, a lover. I find it most admirable, this affection of the family, this lasting reminiscence of the distant relations. We others in Russia, we have it too: we love the parent: but not with so much empressement. I find that trait there altogether essentially English.'

Mrs. Upjohn would have considered the countess 'scarcely respectable,' and would have avoided her acquaintance carefully, unless indeed she happened to be introduced to her by the squire's lady, in which case, of course, her perfect propriety would have been sufficiently guaranteed: but, after all, which of them had the heart the most untainted? To the pure all things are pure: and contrariwise.

So Minna hastened out into those unknown streets of Rome, and by the aid of her self-taught Italian (which was a good deal better than her French, so potent a tutor is love) she soon found her way down the Corso, and off the side alley into the narrow sunless Via Colonna. She followed the numbers down to the familiar eighty-four of Colin's letters, and there she saw upon the door a little painted tin-plate, bearing in English the simple inscription: 'Mr. C. Churchill's Studio.' Minna's heart beat fast for a moment as she mounted the stairs unannounced, and stood within the open door of Colin's modelling room.

A few casts and other sculptor's properties filled up the space between the door and the middle of the studio. Minna paused a second, and looked timidly from behind them at the room beyond. She hardly liked to come forward at once and claim acquaintance: it seemed so strange and unwomanly so to announce herself, now that she had actually got to face it. A certain unwonted bashfulness appeared somehow or other to hold her back; and Minna, who had her little superstitions still, noted it in passing as something ominous. There were two people visible in the studio—both men; and they were talking together quite earnestly, Minna could see, about somebody else who was obviously hidden from her by the Apollo in the foreground. One of them was a very handsome young man in a brown velvet coat, with a loose Rembrandtesque hat of the same stuff stuck with artistic carelessness on one side of his profuse curls: her heart leaped up at once as she recognised with a sudden thrill that that was Colin—— transfigured and glorified a little by success, but still the same dear old Colin as ever, looking the very image of a sculptor, as he stood there, one arm poised lightly on his hip, and turning towards his companion with some wonderful grace that no other race of men save only artists can ever compass. Stop, he was speaking again now; and Minna, all unconscious of listening or prying, bent forward to catch the sound of those precious words as Colin uttered them.

'She's splendid, you know, Winthrop,' Colin was saying enthusiastically, in a voice that had caught a slight Italian trill from Maragliano, unusual on our sterner English lips: 'she's grand, she's beautiful, she's terrible, she's magnificent. Upon my word, in all my life I never yet saw any woman one-half so glorious or so Greek as Cecca. I'm proud of having discovered her; immensely proud. I claim her as my own property, by right of discovery. A lot of other fellows would like to inveigle her away from me; but they won't get her: Cecca's true metal, and she sticks to her original inventor. What a woman she is, really! Now did you ever see such a perfectly glorious arm as that one?'

Minna reeled, almost, as she stood there among the casts and properties, and felt half inclined on the spur of the moment to flee away unseen, and never again speak or write a single word to that perfidious Colin. Cecca, indeed! Cecca! Cecca! Who on earth was this woman Cecca, she would like to know; and what on earth did the faithless Colin ever want with her? Splendid, grand, beautiful, glorious, terrible, magnificent! Oh, Colin, Colin, how could you break her poor little heart so? Should she go back at once to the countess, and not even let Colin know she had ever come to Rome at all to see him? It was too horrible, too sudden, too crushing, too unexpected!

The other man looked towards the unseen Cecca—Minna somehow felt in her heart that Cecca was there, though she couldn't see her—and answered with an almost imperceptible American accent, 'She's certainly very beautiful, Churchill, very beautiful. My dear fellow, I sincerely congratulate you.'

Congratulate you! What! had it come to that? Oh horror! oh shame! had Colin been grossly deceiving her? Had he not only made love in her absence to that black-eyed Italian woman of whom she had always been so much afraid, but had he even made her an offer of marriage, without ever mentioning a word about it to her, Minna? The baseness, the deceit, the wickedness of it! And yet—this Minna thought with a sickening start—was it really base, was it really deceitful, was it really wicked? Colin had never said he would marry her; he had never been engaged to her—oh no, during all those long weary years of doubt and hesitation she had always known he wasn't engaged to her —she had known it, and trembled. Yes, he was free; he was

24

his own master; he could do as he liked: she was only his little cousin Minna: what claim, after all, had she upon him?

At that moment Colin turned, and looked almost towards her, without seeing her. She could have cried out 'Colin!' as she saw his beautiful face and his kindly eyes—too kindly to be untrue, surely—turned nearly upon her; but Cecca, Cecca, the terrible unseen Cecca, somehow restrained her. And Cecca, too, had actually accepted him. Didn't the Yankee man he called Winthrop say, 'I congratulate you'? There was only one meaning possible to put upon such a sentence. Accept him! Why, how could any woman conceivably refuse him? as he moved forward there with his delicate clear-cut face, a face in which the aesthetic temperament stood confessed so unmistakably—Minna could hardly blame this unknown Cecca if she fell in love with him. But for herself—oh, Colin, Cohn, Colin, it was too cruel.

She would at least see Cecca before she stole away unperceived for ever; she would see what manner of woman this was that had enticed away Colin Churchill's love from herself, if indeed he had ever loved her, which was now at least far more than doubtful. So she moved aside gently behind the clay figures, and came in sight of the third person.

It was the exact Italian beauty of her long-nursed girlish terrors! A queenly dark woman, with supple statuesque figure and splendidly set head, was standing before the two young artists in an attitude half studied pose, half natural Calabrian peasant gracefulness. Her brown neck and arms were quite bare; her large limbs were scarcely concealed below by a short and clinging sculpturesque kirtle. She was looking towards Colin with big languishing eyes, and her smile—for she was smiling—had something in it of that sinister air that northerners often notice among even the most beautiful women of the Mediterranean races. It was plain that she couldn't understand what her two admirers were saying in their foreign language; but it was plain also that she knew they were praising her extraordinary beauty, and her eyes flashed forth accordingly with evident pride and overflowing self-satisfaction. Cecca was beautiful, clearly beautiful, both in face and figure, with a rich, mature southern beauty (though in years perhaps she was scarcely twenty), and Minna was forced in spite of herself to admire her form; but she felt instinctively there was something about the girl that she would have feared and dreaded, even if she hadn't heard Colin Churchill speaking of her with such unstinted and unhesitating admiration. So this was Cecca! So this was Cecca! And so this was the end, too, of all her long romantic day-dream!

As she stood there, partly doubting whether to run away or not, Cecca caught sight of her half hidden behind the Apollo, and turning to Colin, cried out sharply in a cold, ringing, musical voice as clear and as cold as crystal, 'See, see; a signorina! She waits to speak with you.'

Colin looked round carelessly, and before Minna could withdraw his eyes met hers in a sudden wonder.

'Minna!' he cried, rushing forward eagerly to meet her, 'Minna! Minna! Why, it must be Minna! How on earth did you manage to get to Rome, little woman? and why on earth didn't you let me know beforehand you were really coming?'

He tried to kiss her as he spoke, but Minna, half doubtful what she ought to do, with swimming brain and tearful eyes, held him off mechanically by withdrawing herself timidly a little, and gave him her hand instead with strange coldness, much to his evident surprise and disappointment.

'She's too modest to kiss me before Winthrop and Cecca,' Colin thought to himself a little nervously; 'but no matter—

26

Winthrop, this is my cousin from England, Miss Wroe, that I've so often spoken to you about.'

His cousin from England! His cousin!! His cousin!!! Ah, yes, that was all he meant by it nowadays clearly. He wanted to kiss her, but merely as a cousin; all his heart, it seemed, was only for this creature he called Cecca, who stood there scowling at her so savagely from under her great heavy eyebrows. He had gone to Rome, as she feared so long ago, and had fallen into the clutches of that dreaded terrible Italian woman.

'Well, Minna,' Colin said, looking at her so tenderly that even Minna herself half believed he must be still in earnest, 'and so you've come to Italy, have you? My dear little girl, why didn't you write and tell me all about it? You've broken in upon me so unexpectedly.' ('So I see,' thought Minna.) 'Why didn't you write and let me know beforehand you were coming to see me?

Minna's heart prompted her inwardly to answer with truth, 'Because I wanted to surprise you, Colin;' but she resisted the natural impulse, much against the grain, and answered instead with marked chilliness, 'Because I didn't know my movements were at all likely to interest you.'

As they two spoke, Hiram Winthrop noticed half unconsciously that Cecca's eyes were steadily riveted upon the newcomer, and that the light within them had changed instantaneously from the quiet gleam of placid self-satisfaction to the fierce glare of rising anger and jealous suspicion.

Colin still held Minna's hand half doubtfully in his, and looked with his open face all troubled into her pretty brown eyes, wondering vaguely what on earth could be the meaning of this unexpected coldness of demeanour.

'Tell me at least how you got here, little woman,' he began again in his soft, gentle voice, with quiet persuasiveness.

'Whatever brought you here, Minna, I'm so glad, so very glad to see you. Tell me how you came, and how long you're going to stop with me.'

Minna sat down blankly on the one chair that stood in the central area of the little studio, not because she wanted to stay there any longer, but because she felt as if her trembling knees were positively giving way beneath her. 'I've taken a place as governess to a Russian girl, Colin,' she answered shortly; 'and I've come to Rome with my pupil's mother.'

Colin felt sure by the faintness of her voice that there was something very serious the matter. 'Minna dearest,' he whispered to her half beneath his breath, 'you aren't well, I'm certain. I'll send away my friend and my model, and then you must tell me all about it, like a dear good little woman.'

Minna started, and her face flushed suddenly again with mounting colour. 'Your model,' she cried, pointing half contemptuously towards the scowling Cecca. 'Your model! Is that woman over there a model, then?'

'Yes, certainly,' Colin answered lightly.

'This lady's a model, Minna. We call her Cecca—that's short for Francesca, you know—and she's my model for a statue of a Spartan maiden I'm now working upon.'

But Cecca, though she couldn't follow the words, had noticed the contemptuous tone and gesture with which Minna had scornfully spoken of 'that woman,' and she knew at once in her hot Italian heart that she stood face to face with a natural enemy. An enemy and a rival. For Cecca, too, had in her own way her small fancies and her bold ambitions.

'She's very beautiful, isn't she?' Hiram Winthrop put in timidly, for he saw with his keen glance that Cecca's handsome face was growing every moment blacker and

28

blacker, and he wanted to avert the coming explosion.

'Well, not so very beautiful to my mind,' Minna answered, with studied coolness, putting her head critically a little on one side, and staring at the model as if she had been made of plaster of Paris; 'though I must say you gentlemen seemed to be admiring her immensely when I came into the room a minute or two ago. I confess she doesn't exactly take my own personal fancy.'

'What is the signorina saying?' Cecca broke in haughtily, in Italian. She felt sure from the scornful tone of Minna's voice that it must at least be something disparaging.

'She says you are beautiful, Signora Cecca,' Colin answered hurriedly, with a sidelong deprecatory glance at Minna. 'Bella bella, bella, bellissima.'

'Bellissima, si, bellissima,' Minna echoed, half frightened, she knew not why; for she felt dimly conscious in her own little mind that they were all three thoroughly afraid in their hearts of the beautiful, imperious Italian woman.

'It is a lie,' Cecca murmured to herself quietly. 4 But it doesn't matter. She was saying that she didn't admire me, and the Englishman and the American tried to stop her. The sorceress! I hate her!'

———————————

CHAPTER XXXI. COUSINS.

They stood all four looking at one another mutely for a few minutes longer, and then Colin broke the ominous silence by saying as politely as he was able, 'Signora Cecca, this lady has come to see me from England, and we are relations. We have not met for many years. Will you excuse my dismissing you for this morning?'

Cecca made a queenly obeisance to Colin, dropped a sort of saucy Italian curtsey to Minna, nodded familiarly to Hiram, and swept out of the studio into the dressing-room without uttering another word.

'She'll go off to Bazzoni's, I'm afraid,' Hiram said, with a sigh of relief, as she shut the door noiselessly and cautiously behind her. 'He's downright anxious to get her, and she's a touchy young woman, that's certain.'

'I'm not at all afraid of that,' Colin answered, smiling; 'she's a great deal too true to me for any such tricks as those, I'm sure, Winthrop. She really likes me, I know, and she won't desert me even for a pique, though I can easily see she's awfully offended.'

'Well, I hope so,' Hiram replied gravely. 'She's far too good a model to be lost. Goodbye, Churchill.—Good morning, Miss Wroe. I hope you'll do me the same honour as you've done your cousin, by coming to take a look some day around my studio.'

'Well, Minna,' Colin said as soon as they were alone, coming up to her and offering once more to kiss her—'why, little woman, what's the matter? Aren't you going to let me kiss you any longer? We always used to kiss one another in the old days, you know, in England.'

'But now we're both of us quite grown up, Colin,' Minna answered, somewhat pettishly, 'so of course that makes all the difference.'

Cohn couldn't understand the meaning of this chilliness; for Minna's late letters, written in the tremor of delight at the surprise she was preparing for him, had been more than usually affectionate; and it would never have entered into his head for a moment to suppose that she could have misinterpreted his remarks about Cecca, even if he had known that she had overheard them. To a sculptor, such criticism of a model, such enthusiasm for the mere form of the shapely human figure, seem so natural and disinterested, so much a necessary corollary of his art, that he never even dreams of guarding against any possible misapprehension. So Colin only bowed his head in silent wonder, and answered slowly, 'But then you know, Minna, we're cousins. Surely there can be no reason why cousins when they meet shouldn't kiss one another.' He couldn't have chosen a worse plea at that particular moment; for as he said it, the blood rushed from Minna's cheeks, and she trembled with excitement at that seeming knell to all her dearest expectations. 'Oh, well, if you put it upon that ground, Colin,' she faltered out half tearfully, 'of course we may kiss one another—as cousins.'

Colin seized her in his arms at the word, and covered her pretty little gipsy face with a string of warm, eager kisses. Even little Minna, in her fright and anxiety, could not help imagining to herself that those were hardly what one could call in fairness mere everyday cousinly embraces. But her evil genius made her struggle to release herself, according to the code of etiquette which she had learnt as becoming from her friends and early companions; and she pushed Colin away after a moment's doubtful acquiescence, with a little petulant gesture of half-affected anger. The philosophic observer may indeed note that among the English people

31

only women of the very highest breeding know how to let themselves be kissed by their lovers with becoming and unresisting dignity. Tennyson's Maud, when her cynic admirer kissed her for the first time, 'took the kiss sedately.' I fear it must be admitted that under the same circumstances Minna Wroe, dear little native-born lady though she was, would have felt it incumbent upon her as a woman and a maiden to resist and struggle to the utmost of her power.

As for Colin, having got rid of that first resistance easily enough, he soon settled in his own mind to his own entire satisfaction that Minna had been only a little shy of him after so long an absence, and had perhaps been playing off a sort of mock-modest coyness upon him, in order to rouse him to an effective aggression. So he said no more to her about the matter, but asked her full particulars as to her new position and her journey; and even Minna herself, disappointed as she was, could not help opening out her full heart to dear old Colin, and telling him all about everything that had happened to her in the last six weeks, except her inner hopes and fears and lamentations. Yes, she had come to Rome to live—she didn't say 'on purpose to be near you, Colin'—and they would have abundant opportunities of seeing one another frequently; and Madame was very kind, for an employer, you know—as employers go—you can't expect much, of course, from an employer. And Colin showed her all his busts and statues; and Minna admired them profoundly with a genuine admiration. And then, what prices he got for them! Why, Colin, really nowadays you're become quite a gentleman! And Colin, to whom that social metamorphosis had long grown perfectly familiar, laughed heartily at the naïve remark and then looked round with a touch of professional suspicion, for fear some accidental patron might have happened to come in and overhear the simple little confession. Altogether, their conversation got very close and affectionate and cousinly.

At last, after they had talked about everything that most concerned them both, save only the one thing that concerned them both more than anything, Minna asked in as unconcerned a tone as she could muster up, 'And this model, Colin—Cecca, I think you called her—what of her?'

Colin's eye lighted up with artistic enthusiasm as he answered warmly, 'Oh, she's the most beautiful girl in all Rome, little woman. I found her out by accident last year, at a village in Calabria where Winthrop and I had gone for a Christmas holiday; and I induced her to come to Rome and go in for a model's life as a profession. Isn't she just magnificent, Minna?'

'Very magnificent indeed, I dare say,' Minna answered coldly; 'but not to my mind by any means pleasing.'

'I wonder you think that,' Colin said in frank astonishment: for he was too much a sculptor even to suspect that Minna could take any other view of his model except the purely artistic one. 'She was the original of that Nymph Bathing of mine that you see over yonder.'

Minna looked critically at the Nymph Bathing—a shameless hussy, truly, if ever there was one—and answered in a chilly voice, 'I like it the least of all your statues, if you care to have my opinion, Colin.'

'Well, now, I'm awfully sorry for that, Minna,' Colin went on seriously, regarding the work with that despondent eye with which one always views one's own performances after hearing by any chance an adverse criticism; 'for I rather liked the nymph myself, you know, and I can generally rely upon your judgment as being about the very best to be had anywhere in the open market. There's no denying, little woman, that you've got a born taste somehow or other for the art of sculpture.'

If only women would say what they mean to us! but they won't, so what's the use of bothering one's head about it?

33

They'll make themselves and us unhappy for a twelvemonth together—lucky indeed if not for ever—by petting and fretting over some jealous fancy or other, some vague foolish suspicion, which, if they would but speak out frankly for a moment, might be dispelled and settled with a good hearty kiss in half a second. Our very unsuspiciousness, our masculine downrightness and definiteness, make us slow to perceive their endless small tiffs and crooked questions; slow to detect the real meaning that underlies their unaccountable praise and blame of other people, given entirely from the point of view of their own marvellous subjective universe. The question whether Cecca was handsome or otherwise was to Colin Churchill a simple question of external aesthetics; he was as unprejudiced about it as he would have been in judging a Greek torso or a modern Italian statue. But to Minna it was mainly a question between her own heart and Colin's. If she had only told him then and there her whole doubt and trouble —confessed it, as a man would have confessed it, openly and simply, and asked at once for a straightforward explanation, she would have saved herself long weeks of misery and self-torture and internal questionings. But she did not; and Colin, never doubting her misapprehension, dropped the matter lightly as one of no practical importance whatsoever.

So it came to pass that Minna let that first day at Rome slip by without having come to any understanding at all with Colin; and went home to Madame's still in doubt in her own troubled little mind whether or not she was really and truly quite engaged to him. Did he love her, or did he merely like her? Was she his sweetheart, or merely an old friend whom he had known and confided in ever since those dim old days at Wootton Mandeville? Minna could have cried her eyes out over that abstruse and difficult personal question. And Colin never even knew that the question had for one moment so much as once occurred to her.

'I may have one more kiss before you go, little woman,' Colin said to her tenderly, as she was on the point of leaving. Minna's eyes glistened brightly. 'One more kiss, you know, dear, for old times' sake, Minna.' Minna's eyes filled with tears, and she could hardly brush them away without his perceiving it. It was only for old times' sake, then, for old times' sake, not for love and the future. Oh, Colin, Colin, how bitter! how bitter!

'As a cousin, Colin?' she murmured interrogatively.

Cohn laughed a gay little laugh. 'Strictly as a cousin,' he answered merrily, lingering far longer on her lips, however, than the most orthodox cousinly affection could ever possibly have sufficed to justify.

Minna sighed and jumped away hastily. That night, in her own room, looking at Colin's photograph, and thinking of the dreadful Italian woman, and all the dangers that beset her round about, she muttered to herself ever so often, 'Strictly as a cousin, he said *strictly* as a cousin—for old times' sake—strictly as a cousin.'

There was only one real comfort left for her in all the dreary, gloomy, disappointing outlook. At least that horrid high-born Miss Gwen Howard-Russell (ugh, what a name!) had disappeared bodily altogether from off the circle of Cohn's horizon.

CHAPTER XXXII. RE-ENTER GWEN.

Lothrop Audouin and Hiram Winthrop were strolling arm in arm together down the Corso.

Audouin had just arrived from Paris, having crossed from America only a week earlier.

Four years had made some difference in his personal appearance; his beard and hair were getting decidedly grizzled, and for the first time in his life Hiram noticed that his friend seemed to have aged a great deal faster and more suddenly than he himself had. But Audouin's carriage was still erect and very elastic; there was plenty of life and youth about him yet, plenty even of juvenile fire and originality.

'It's very disappointing certainly, Hiram,' he said, as they turned into the great thoroughfare of the city together, 'this delay in getting your talents recognised: but I have faith in you still; and to faith, you know, as the Hebrew preacher said, all things are possible. The great tardigrade world is hard to move; you need the pou sto of a sensation to get in the thin edge of your Archimedean lever. But the recognition will come, as sure as the next eclipse; meanwhile, my dear fellow, you must go on working in faith, and I surmise that in the end you will move mountains. If not Soracte just at once, my friend, well at any rate to begin upon the Monte Testaccio.'

Hiram smiled half sadly. 'But I haven't faith, you know, Mr. Audouin,' he answered, in as easy a tone as he could well muster. 'I begin to regard myself in the dismal light of a portentous failure. Like Peter, I feel myself sinking in the water, and have no one to take me by the hand and lift me out of it.'

Audouin answered only by an airy wave of his five

delicate outspread fingers. 'And Miss Russell?' he asked after half a second's pause. 'Has she come to Rome yet? You know she said she would be here this winter.'

As he spoke, he looked deep into Hiram's eyes with so much meaning that Hiram felt his face grow hot, and thought to himself, 'What a wonderful man Mr. Audouin is, really! In spite of all my silence and reserve he has somehow managed to read my innermost secret. How could he ever have known that Miss Russell's was the hand I needed to lift me out of the Sea of Gennesaret!'

But how self-contained and self-centred even the best of us are at bottom! for Audouin only meant to change the subject, and the deep look in his eyes when he spoke about Gwen to Hiram had reference entirely to his own heart and not to his companion's.

'I haven't seen or heard anything of her yet,' Hiram answered shyly, 'but the season has hardly begun so far, and I calculate we may very probably find her at Rome in the course of the next fortnight.'

'How he looks down and hesitates!' Audouin thought to himself in turn as Hiram answered him. 'How on earth can he have succeeded in discovering and recognising my unspoken secret?'

So we walk this world together, cheek by jowl, yet all at cross purposes, each one thinking mainly of himself, and at the same time illogically fancying that his neighbour is not all equally engrossed on his own similarly important personality. We imagine he is always thinking about us, but he is really doing quite otherwise—thinking about himself exactly as we are.

They walked on a few steps further in silence, each engaged in musing on his own thoughts, and then suddenly a voice came from a jeweller's shop by the corner, 'Oh, papa, just look! Mr. Audouin and his friend the painter.'

As Gwen Howard-Russell uttered those simple words, two hearts went beating suddenly faster on the pavement outside, each after its own fashion. Audouin heard chiefly his own name, and thought to himself gladly, 'Then she has not forgotten me.' Hiram heard chiefly the end of the sentence, and thought to himself bitterly, 'And shall I never be more to her then than merely that—"his friend the painter"?'

'Delighted to see you, Mr. Audouin,' the colonel said stiffly, in a voice which at once belied its own spoken welcome. 'And you too, Mr.—ur—Mr. ————'

'Winthrop, papa,' Gwen suggested blandly; and Hiram was grateful to her even for remembering it.

'Winthrop, of course,' the colonel accepted with a decorous smile, as who should gracefully concede that Hiram had no doubt a sort of right in his own small way to some kind of cognomen or other. 'And are you still painting, Mr. Winthrop?'

'I am,' Hiram answered shortly. [The subject was one that did not interest him.] 'And you, Miss Russell? Have you come here to spend the winter?'

'Oh yes,' Gwen replied, addressing herself, however, rather to Audouin than to Hiram. 'You see we haven't forgotten our promise. But we're not stopping at the hotel this time, we're at the Villa Panormi—just outside the town, you know, on the road to the Ponte Molle.

A cousin of ours, a dear stupid old fellow——'

'Gwen, my dear! now really you know—the Earl of Beaminster, Mr. Audouin.'

'Yes, that's his name; Lord Beaminster, and a dear old stupid as ever was born, too, I can tell you. Well, he's taken the Villa Panormi for the season; it belongs to some poor wretched creature of a Roman prince, I believe (his grandfather was lackey to a cardinal), who's in want of money dreadfully, and he lets it to my cousin to go and gamble away the proceeds at Monte Carlo. It's just outside the Porta del Popolo, about a mile off; and the gardens are really quite delightful. You must both of you come there very often to see us.'

'But really, Gwen, we must ask Beaminster first, you know, before we begin introducing our friends to him,' the colonel interjected apologetically, casting down a furtive and uneasy glance at Hiram's costume, which certainly displayed a most admired artistic disorder. 'We ought to send him to call first at Mr.—ur—Winthrop's studio.'

'Of course,' Gwen answered. 'And so he shall go this very afternoon, if I tell him to. The dear old stupid always does whatever I order him.'

'If we continue to take up the pavement in this way,' Audouin put in gravely, 'we shall get taken up ourselves by the active and intelligent police officers of a redeemed Italy. Which way are you going now, Miss Russell? towards the Piazza? Then we'll go with you if you will allow us.— Hiram, my dear fellow, if you'll permit me to suggest it, it's very awkward walking four abreast on these narrow Roman side-walks—pavements, I mean; forgive the Americanism, Miss Russell. Yes, that's better so. And when did you and the colonel come to Rome. Now tell me?'

In a moment, much to Hiram's chagrin, and the colonel's too, Audouin had managed to lead the way, tête-à-tête with Gwen, shuffling off the two others to follow behind, and get along as best they might in the background together. Now the colonel was not a distinguished conversationalist, and Hiram was hardly in a humour for talking, so after they had interchanged a few harmless conventionalities and a mild platitude or two about the weather, they both relapsed into moody silence, and occupied themselves by catching a scrap every now and then of what Gwen and Audouin were saying in front of them.

'And that very clever Mr. Churchill, too, Mr. Audouin! I hear he's getting on quite wonderfully. Lord Beaminster bought one of his groups, you know, and brought him into fashion—partly by my pushing, I must confess, to be quite candid—and now, I'm told, he's commanding almost any price he chooses to ask in the way of sculpture. We haven't seen him yet, of course, but I mean papa and my cousin to look him up in his own quarters at the very earliest opportunity.'

'Oh, a clever enough young artist, certainly, but not really, Miss Russell, half so genuine an artist in feeling as my friend Win-throp.'

Hiram could have fallen on his neck that moment for that half-unconscious piece of kindly recommendation.

A few steps further they reached the corner of the Via de' Condotti, and Gwen paused for a second as she looked across the street, with a little sudden cry of recognition. A handsome young man was coming round the corner from the Piazza di Spagna, with a gipsy-looking girl leaning lightly on his arm, and talking to him with much evident animation. It was Colin and Minna, going out together on Minna's second holiday, to see the wonders of the Vatican and St. Peter's.

'Mr. Churchill!' Gwen cried, coming forward cordially to meet him. 'What a delightful rencontre! We were just talking of you.

And here are other friends, you see, besides—Mr. Winthrop, my father, and Mr. Audouin.' Minna stood half aside in a little embarrassment, wondering who on earth the grand lady could be (she had penetration enough to recognise at once that she *was* a grand lady) talking so

41

familiarly with our Colin.

'Miss Howard-Russell!' Colin cried on his side, taking her hand warmly. 'Then you've come back again! I'm so glad to see you! And you too, Mr. Audouin; this is really a great pleasure.—Miss Russell, I owe you so many thanks. It was you, I believe, who sent my first patron, Lord Beaminster, to visit my studio.'

'Oh, don't speak of it, please, Mr. Churchill. It's we who owe *you* thanks rather, for the pleasure your beautiful group of Autumn has given us. And dear stupid old Lord Beaminster used to amuse everybody so much by telling them how he wanted you to put a clock-dial in the place of the principal figure, until I managed at last to laugh him out of it. I made his life a burden to him, I assure you, by getting him to see how very ridiculous it was of him to try to spoil your lovely composition.'

They talked for a minute or two longer at the street corner, Gwen explaining once more to Colin how she and the colonel had come as Lord Beaminster's guests to the Villa Panormi; and meanwhile poor little Minna stood there out in the cold, growing redder every second, and boiling over with indignation to think that that horrid Miss Howard-Russell should have dropped down upon them from the clouds at the very wrong moment, just on purpose to make barefaced love so openly to her Colin.

It was Gwen herself, however, who first took notice of Minna, whom she saw standing a little apart, and looking very much out of it indeed among so many greetings of old acquaintances. 'And your friend?' she said to Colin kindly. 'You haven't introduced her to us yet. May we have the pleasure?' And she took a step forward with womanly gentleness to relieve the poor girl from her obvious embarrassment.

'Excuse me, Minna dear,' Colin said, taking her hand and

leading her forward quietly.

'My cousin, Miss Wroe: Miss Howard-Bussell, Colonel Howard-Russell, Mr. Audouin, Mr. Winthrop.'

Minna bowed to them all stiffly with cheeks burning, and then fell back again at once angrily into her former position.

'And have you come to Rome lately, Miss Wroe?' Gwen asked of her with genuine kindness. 'Are you here on a visit to your cousin, whose work we all admire so greatly?'

'I came a week ago,' Minna answered defiantly, blurting out the whole truth (lest she should seem to be keeping back anything) and pitting her whole social nonentity, as it were, against the grand lady's assured position.

'I came a week ago; and I'm a governess to a little Russian girl here; and I'm going to stop all the winter.'

'That'll be very nice for all of us,' Gwen put in softly, with a look that might almost have disarmed Minna's hasty suspicions. 'And how exceedingly pleasant for you to have your cousin here, too! I suppose it was partly on that account, now, that you decided upon coming here?'

'It was,' Minna answered shortly, without vouchsafing any further explanation.

'And where are you going now, Mr. Churchill?' Gwen asked, seeing that Minna was clearly not in a humour for conversation. 'Are you showing your cousin the sights of Rome, I wonder?'

'Exactly what I am doing, Miss Russell. We're going now to see the Vatican.'

'Oh, then, do let us come with you! I should like to go too. I do love going through the galleries with an artist who can tell one all about them!'

'But, Gwen, my dear, Beaminster's lunch hour——

'Oh, bother Lord Beaminster's lunch hour, papa! Hire somebody to go and tell him we've been detained and can't possibly be back by lunch-time. I want to go and see the Vatican, and improve the opportunity of making Miss Wroe's better acquaintance.' Minna bowed again with bitter mock solemnity.

So they all went to the Vatican, spoiling poor little Minna's holiday that had begun so delightfully (for she and Colin had talked quite like old times on their way from the Via Clementina), and tiring themselves out with strolling up and down those eye-distracting corridors and galleries. It was a queer game of cross questions and crooked answers all round between them. Audouin, flashing gaily as of old, and scintillating every now and then with little bits of crisp criticism over pictures or statues, was trying all the time to get a good talk with Gwen Howard-Russell, and to oust from her side the unconscious Colin. Gwen, smiling benignly at Audouin's quaintly worded sallies, was doing her best to call out Colin's opinions upon all the works in the Vatican off-hand. Hiram, only anxious to avoid being bored by the Colonel's vapid remarks upon the things he saw (he called Raphaels and Guidos and Titians alike 'pretty, very pretty'), was chiefly engaged in overhearing the conversation of the others. And Minna, poor little Minna, to whom Colin paid as much assiduous attention as the circumstances permitted, was longing all the time to steal away and have a good cry about the horrid goings on of that abominable Miss Howard-Russell.

From the minute Minna had seen Gwen, and heard what manner of things Gwen had to say to Colin, she forgot straightway all her fears about the Italian Cecca creature, and recognised at once with a woman's instinct that her real danger lay in Gwen, and in Gwen only. It was with Gwen that Colin was likely to fall in love; Gwen, with her grand manners and her high-born face and her fine relations, and her insinuating, intoxicating adulation. How she made up to him and praised him! How she talked to him about his

44

genius and his love of beauty! How she tried to flatter him up before her own very face! Miss Gwen was beautiful; that much Minna couldn't help grudgingly admitting. Miss Gwen had a delightful self-possession and calmness about her that Minna would have given the world to have rivalled. Miss Gwen had everything in her favour. No wonder Colin was so polite and courteous to her; no wonder poor little trembling Minna was really nowhere at all beside her. And then she had done Colin a great service; she had recommended Lord Beaminster and many other patrons to go and see his studio. Ah me! how sad little Minna felt that evening when she tried to compare her own small chances with those of great, grand, self-possessed Miss Howard-Russell! If only Cohn loved her! But he had as good as said himself that he didn't love her—not worth speaking of: he had said he kissed her 'strictly as a cousin.'

As Gwen and the colonel drove back in a hired botto to the Villa Panormi in the cool of the evening, Gwen said to her papa quite innocently, 'What a charming young man that delightful Mr. Churchill is really! Did. you notice how kind and attentive he was to that funny little cousin of his in the brown bonnet? Only a governess, you know, come to Rome with a Russian family; and yet he made as much of her, almost, as he did of you and me and Mr. Audouin! So thoughtful and good of him, I call it; but there—he's always such a perfect gentleman. I dare say that's the daughter of some washerwoman or somebody down at Wootton Mandeville, and he pays her quite as much attention as if she were actually a countess or a duchess.'

'You don't seem to remember, Gwen,' the colonel answered grimly, 'that his own father was only a kitchen gardener, and that he himself began life, I understand, as a common stonecutter.'

'Nonsense!' Gwen replied energetically.

'*You* seem to forget on the other hand, papa, that he was born a great sculptor, and that genius is after all the only true nobility.'

'It wasn't so when I was a boy,' the colonel continued, with a grim smile; 'and I fancy it isn't so yet, Gwen, in our own country, whatever these precious Yankee friends of yours may choose to tell you.'

CHAPTER XXXIII. CECCA.

A fortnight later, Signora Cecca walked sulkily down the narrow staircase of the handsome Englishman's little studio. Signora Cecca was evidently indulging herself in the cheap luxury of a very bad humour. To an Italian woman of Cecca's peculiarly imperious temperament, indulgence in that congenial exercise of the spleen may be looked upon as a real and genuine luxury. Cecca brooded over her love and her wrath and her jealousy as thwarted children brood over their wrongs in the solitude of the bedroom where they have been sent to expiate some small everyday domestic offence in silence and loneliness. The handsome Englishman had then a sweetheart, an innamorata, in his own country, clearly; and now she had come to Rome, the perfidious creature, on purpose to visit him. That was a contingency that Cecca had never for one moment counted upon when she left her native village in Calabria and followed the unknown sculptor obediently to Rome, where she rose at once to be the acknowledged queen of the artists' models.

Not that Cecca had ever seriously thought, on her own part, of marrying Colin. Mother of heaven, no! for the handsome Englishman was a heretic and a foreigner; and to marry him would have been utterly shocking to all Cecca's deepest and most ingrained moral and religious feelings. For Cecca was certainly by no means devoid of principle. She would have stuck a knife into you in a quarrel as soon as look at you: she would have poisoned a rival remorselessly in cold blood under the impelling influence of treacherous Italian jealousy without a moment's hesitation, but she would have decidedly drawn a sharp line at positively marrying a foreigner and a heretic. No, she didn't want to marry Colin. But she wanted to keep him to herself as her own private and particular possession: she wanted to have him for her own without external interference: she wanted to prevent all other women from having anything to say or to do with her own magnificent handsome Englishman. He needn't marry *her*, of course, but he certainly mustn't be allowed to go and marry any other woman.

'If I were a jealous fool,' Cecca thought to herself in her own vigorous Calabrian patois, 'I should run away and leave him outright, and make Bazzoni's fortune all at once by letting him model from me. But I'm not a jealous fool, and I don't want, as the proverb says, to cut off my own right hand merely in order to fling it in the face of my rival. The English signorina loves the handsome Englishman — that's certain. Then, mother of God, the English signorina will have to pay for it. Dear little Madonna della Guardia, help me to cook her stew for her, and you shall have tapers, ever so many tapers, and a couple of masses too in your own little chapel on the headland at Monteleone. There is no Madonna so helpful at a pinch as our own Madonna della Guardia at Monteleone. Besides, she isn't too particular. She will give you her aid on an emergency, and not be so very angry with you after all, because you've had to go a little bit out of your way, perhaps, to effect your purpose. Blood of St. Elmo, no: she took candles from the good uncle when he shot the carabiniere who came to take him up over the affair of the ransom of the American traveller; and she protected him well for the candles too, and he has never been arrested for it even to this very minute.

The English signorina had better look out, by Bacchus, if she wants to meddle with Cecca Bianchelli and Madonna della Guardia at Monteleone. Besides, she's nothing but a heretic herself, if it comes to that, so what on earth, I should like to know, do the blessed saints in heaven care for her?'

48

Signora Cecca stood still for a moment in the middle of the Via Colonna, and asked herself this question passionately, with a series of gesticulations which in England might possibly have excited unfavourable attention. For example, she set her teeth hard together, and drew an imaginary knife deliberately across the throat of an equally imaginary aerial rival. But in Rome, where people are used to gesticulations, nobody took the slightest notice of them.

'She has been four times to the studio already,' Signora Cecca went on to herself, resuming her homeward walk as quietly as if nothing at all had intervened to diversify it: 'and every time she comes the handsome Englishman talks to her, makes love to her, fondles her almost before my very eyes. And she, the basilisk, she loves him too, though she pretends to be so very coy and particular: she loves him: she cannot deceive me: I saw it at once, and I see it still through all her silly transparent pretences. She cannot take in Cecca Bianchelli and Madonna della Guardia at Monteleone. She loves him, the Saracen, and she shall answer for it. No other woman but me shall ever dare to love the handsome Englishman.

'The other English signorina, to be sure, she loves him too: but then, pooh, I don't care for her, I don't mind her, I'm not afraid of her. The Englishman doesn't love her, that's certain. She's too cold and white-faced. He loves the little one. The little one is prettier; she has life in her features; she might almost be an Italian girl, only she's too insipid. She shall answer for his loving her. I hate her; and the dear little Madonna shall have her candles.'

As she walked along, a young man in a Roman workman's dress came up to her wistfully, and looked in her face with a doubtful expression of bashful timidity. 'Good morning, Signora Cecca,' he said, with curiously marked politeness. 'You come from the Englishman's studio, I suppose? You have had a sitting?'

Cecca looked up at him haughtily and coldly. 'You again, Giuseppe,' she said, with a toss of her beautiful head and a curl of her lip like a tragedy Cleopatra. 'And what do you want with me? You're always bothering me now about something or other, on the strength of some slight previous boyish acquaintance.'

The young man smiled her back an angry smile, Italian fashion. 'It's Giuseppe now, I suppose,' he said, with a sniff: 'it used to be Beppo down there yonder at Monteleone. I shall have to take to calling you in your turn "Signora Francesca," I'm thinking: you've grown too fine for me since you came to Rome and got among your rich sculptor acquaintances. A grand trade indeed, to sit half the day, half uncovered, in a studio for a pack of Englishmen to take your figure and make statues of you! I liked you far better, myself, when you poured the wine out long ago at the osteria by the harbour at Monteleone.'

Cecca looked up at him once more haughtily. 'You did?' she said. 'You did, did you? Well, that was all very well for a fellow like you, only fit to tend a horse or chop up rotten olive roots for firewood. But for me that sort of life didn't answer. I prefer Rome, and fame, and art, and plenty.' And as she said the last words she clinked the cheap silver bracelets that she wore upon her arm, and touched the thin gold brooch that fastened up the light shawl thrown coquettishly across her shapely shoulders.

'You don't,' Giuseppe answered boldly.

'You are not happy here, Cecca mia, as you were at Monteleone. You worry your heart out about your Englishman, and he does not love you. What does he think of you or care for you? You are to him merely a model, a thing to mould clay from; no more than the draperies and

50

the casts that he works with so carelessly in his studio. And it is for that that you throw me over—me, Beppo, who loved you always so dearly at Monteleone.'

Cecca looked at him and laughed lightly. '*You*, Beppo!' she cried, as if amused and surprised. 'You, my friend! You thought to marry Cecca Bianchelli! Oh no, little brother; that would be altogether too ridiculous. There is no model in Rome, do you know, who has such a figure or earns so much money as I do.'

'But you loved me once, or at least you said so, Signora Francesca.'

'And you should hear how the excellencies admire me, and call me beautiful, Signor Giuseppe.'

'Cecca, Cecca, you know I have come to Rome for your sake only. I don't want you to love me, I only want to see you and be near you. Won't you let me come and see you this evening?'

'Very sorry, Signor Giuseppe. It would have given me the deepest satisfaction, but I have a prior engagement. A painter of my acquaintance takes me to the Circo Beale.'

'But, Cecca, Cecca!'

'Well, Beppo?'

'Ah, that is good, "Beppo." You relent then, Signora?'

'As between old friends, Signor Giuseppe, one may use the diminutive.'

'And you will let me come then tomorrow night and see you for half an hour—for half an hour only, Cecca?'

'Well, you were a good friend of mine once, and I have need of you for a project of my own, at the moment. Yes, you may come if you like, Beppo.'

'Ten thousand thanks, Signora. You are busy, I will not keep you. Good evening, Cecca.'

51

'Good evening, my friend. You are a good fellow after all, Beppo. Good evening.'

CHAPTER XXXIV. HIRAM SEES LAND.

U pon my word,' Gwen Howard-Russell thought to herself in the gardens of the Villa Panormi, 'I really can't understand that young Mr. Churchill. He's four years older, and he ought to be four years wiser now, than when we were last at Rome, but he's actually just as stupid and as dull of comprehension as ever; he positively doesn't see when a girl's in love with him. He must be utterly bound up in his sculpture and his artistic notions, that's what it is, or else he'd surely discover what one was driving at when one gives him every possible sort of opportunity. One would have thought he'd have seen lots of society during these four winters that he's been comparatively famous, and that he would have found out what people mean when they say such things to him. But he hasn't, and I declare he's really more polite and attentive even now to that little governess cousin of his, with the old-fashioned bonnet, than he is to me myself, in spite of everything.'

For it had never entered into Gwen's heart to think that Colin might possibly be in love himself with the little gipsy-faced governess cousin.

'Cousin Dick,' Gwen said a few minutes later to Lord Beaminster, 'I've asked Mr. Churchill and my two Americans to come up and have a cup of tea with us this afternoon out here in the garden.'

'Certainly, my dear,' the earl answered, smiling with all his false teeth most amiably; 'the house is your own, you know. (And, by George, she makes it so, certainly without asking me. But who on earth could ever be angry with such a splendid high-spirited creature?) Bring your Americans here by all means, and give that man with the outlandish name plenty of tea, please, to keep him quiet. By Jove, Gwen, I never can understand for the life of me what the dickens the fellow's talking about.'

In due time the guests arrived, and Gwen, who had determined by this time to play a woman's last card, took great care during the whole afternoon to talk as much as possible to Hiram and as little as possible to Colin Churchill. She was determined to let him think he had a rival; that is the surest way of making a man discover whether he really cares for a woman or otherwise.

'Oh yes, I've been to Mr. Winthrop's studio,' she said in answer to Audouin's inquiry, 'and we admired so much a picture of a lake with such a funny name to it, didn't we, papa? It was really beautiful, Mr. Winthrop. I've never seen anything of yours that I've been pleased with so much. Don't you think it splendid, Mr. Audouin?'

'A fine picture in its way—yes, certainly, Miss Russell; but not nearly so good, to my thinking, as the Capture of Babylon he's now working on.'

'You think so, really? Well, now, for my part I like the landscape better. There's so much more originality and personality in it, I fancy. Mr. Winthrop, which do you yourself like the best of your performances?'

Hiram blushed with pleasure. Gwen had never before taken so much notice of him. 'I'm hardly a good judge myself,' he faltered out timidly. 'I wouldn't for worlds pit my own small opinion, of course, against Mr. Audouin's. I'm trying my best at the Capture of Babylon, naturally, but I don't seem to satisfy my own imaginary standard in historical painting, somehow, nearly as well as in external nature. For my own part, I like the landscapes best. I quite agree with you, Miss Russell, that Lake Chattawauga is about my high-water mark.'

('Lake Chattawauga!' the earl interjected pensively—but

54

nobody took the slightest notice of him. 'Lake Chattawauga! Do you really mean to say you've painted the picture of a place with such a name as Lake Chattawauga? I should suppose it must be somewhere or other over in America.')

'I'm so glad to hear you say so,' Gwen answered cordially, 'because one's always wrong, you know, in matters of art criticism; and it's such a comfort to hear that one may be right now and again if only by accident. I liked Lake Chattawauga quite immensely; I don't know when I've seen a picture that pleased me so much, Mr. Winthrop. — What do you say, Mr. Churchill?'

'I think you and Winthrop are quite right, Miss Russell. His landscapes are very, very pretty, and I wish he'd devote himself to them entirely, and give up historical painting and figure subjects altogether.'

('The first time I ever noticed a trace of professional jealousy in young Churchill,' thought Audouin to himself sapiently. 'He doesn't want Hiram, apparently, to go on with the one thing which is certain to lead him in the end to fame and fortune.')

'And there was a lovely little sketch of a Tyrolese waterfall,' Gwen began again enthusiastically. 'Wasn't it exquisite, papa? You know you said you'd so much like to buy it for the dining-room.'

Hiram flushed again. 'I'm so glad you liked my little things,' he said, trembling with delight. 'I didn't think you cared in the least for any of my work, Miss Russell. I was afraid you weren't at all interested in the big canvases.'

'Not like your work, Mr. Winthrop!' Gwen cried, with half a glance aside at Colin. 'Oh yes, I've always admired it most sincerely! Why, don't you remember, our friendship with you and Mr. Audouin began just with my admiring a little water-colour you were making the very first day I ever saw you, by the Lake of the Thousand Islands?' (Hiram nodded a joyful assent. Why, how could he ever possibly forget it?) 'And then you know there was that beautiful little sketch of the Lago Albano, that you gave me the day I was leaving Italy last. I have it hung up in our drawing-room at home in England, and I think it's one of the very prettiest pictures I ever looked at.'

Hiram could have cried like a child that moment with the joy and excitement of a long pent-up nature.

And so, through all that delightful afternoon, Gwen kept leading up, without intermission, to Hiram Winthrop. Hiram himself hardly knew what on earth to make of it. Gwen was very kind and polite to him to-day—that much was certain; and that, at least, was quite enough to secure Hiram an unwonted amount of genuine happiness. How he hugged himself over her kindly smiles and appreciative criticisms! How he fancied in his heart, with tremulous hesitation, that she really was beginning to care just a little bit for him, were it ever so little! In short, for the moment, he was in the seventh heaven, and he felt happier than he had ever felt before in his whole poor, wearisome, disappointed lifetime.

When they were going away, Gwen said once to Hiram (holding his hand in hers just a second longer than was necessary too, he fancied), 'Now, remember, you must come again and see us very soon, Mr. Winthrop—and you too, Mr. Audouin. We want you both to come as often as you're able, for we're quite dull out here in the country, so far away from the town and the Corso.' But she never said a single word of that sort to Cohn Churchill, who was standing close beside them, and heard it all, and thought to himself, 'I wonder whether Miss Russell has begun to take a fancy at last to our friend Winthrop? He's a good fellow, and after all she couldn't do better if she were to search diligently through the entire British peerage.' So utterly had Gwen's wicked little ruse failed of its deceitful, jealous intention.

But as they walked Rome-ward together, to the Porta del Popolo, Audouin said at last musingly to Hiram, 'Miss Russell was in a very gracious mood this afternoon, wasn't she, my dear fellow?'

He looked at Hiram so steadfastly while he said it that Hiram almost blushed again, for he didn't like to hear the subject mentioned, however guardedly, before a third person like Colin Churchill. 'Yes,' he answered shyly, 'she spoke very kindly indeed about my little landscapes. I had no idea before that she really thought anything about them. And how good of her, too, to keep my water-colour of the Lago Albano in her own drawing-room!'

Audouin smiled a gently cynical little Bostonian smile, and answered nothing.

'How strangely one-sided and egotistic we are, after all!' he thought to himself quietly as he walked along. 'We think each of ourselves, and never a bit of other people. Hiram evidently fancied that Miss Russell—Gwen—why not call her so?—wanted *him* to come again to the Villa Panormi. A moment's reflection might have shown him that she couldn't possibly have asked *me*, without at the same time asking *him* also! And it was very clever of her, too, to invite him first, so as not to make the invitation look quite too pointed. She was noticeably kind to Hiram to-day, because he's my protégé. But Hiram, with all his strong, good qualities, is not keen-sighted—not deep enough to fathom the profound abysses of a woman's diplomacy! I don't believe even now he sees what she was driving at. But *I* know: I feel certain I know; I can't be mistaken. It was a very good sign, too, a very good sign, that though she asked me (and of course Hiram with me) to come often to the villa, she didn't think in the least of asking that young fellow Churchill. It's a terribly presumptuous thing to fancy you have won such a woman's heart as Gwen Howard-Russell's; but I imagine I must be right this time. I don't believe I can possibly be mistaken any longer. The convergence of the evidences is really quite too overwhelming.'

CHAPTER XXXV. MAN PROPOSES.

Ten days had passed, and during those ten days Gwen had met both Hiram and Colin on two or three occasions. Each time she saw them together she was careful to talk a great deal more with the young American than with his English companion. At last, one Sunday afternoon, both the young men 'had gone out to the Villa Panormi with Audouin, for a cup of afternoon tea in the garden; and after tea was over, they had stolen away in pairs down the long alleys of oranges, and among the broken statues and tazzas filled with flowers upon the mouldering balustraded Italian terraces. 'Come with me, Mr. Winthrop,' Gwen cried gaily to Hiram (with a side glance at Colin once more to see how he took it). 'I want to show you such a lovely spot for one of your pretty little watercolour sketches—a bower of clematis, with such great prickly pears and aloes for the foreground, that I'm sure you'll fall in love with the whole picture the moment you see it.'

Hiram followed her gladly down to the arbour, a little corner at the bottom of the garden, rather English than Italian in its first conception, but thickly overgrown with tangled masses of sub-tropical vegetation. It's very pretty,' he said, 'certainly very pretty. Just the sort of thing that Mr. Audouin would absolutely revel in.'

'Shall I call him?' Gwen asked, going to the door of the arbour and looking about her carelessly. 'He must be somewhere or other hereabout.'

'Oh no, don't, Miss Russell,' Hiram answered hastily. 'He's having a long talk with Churchill about art, from what I overheard. Don't disturb them. Mr. Audouin has a wonderful taste in art, you know: I love to hear him talk about it in his own original pellucid fashion.'

'You're very fond of him, aren't you?' Gwen asked, looking at him with her big beautiful eyes. 'Is he any relation of yours?' 'Relation!' Hiram cried, 'oh dear no, Miss Bussell. But he's been so kind to me, so very kind to me! You can't imagine how much I owe to Mr. Audouin.'

He said it so earnestly, and seemed to want so much to talk about him, that Gwen sat down upon the stone seat in the little arbour and answered with womanly interest, 'Tell me all about it, then, Mr. Winthrop. I should like to hear how you came to pick up with him.'

Thus encouraged, Hiram, to his own immense astonishment, let loose the floodgates of his pent-up speech, and began to narrate the whole story of his lonely childhood, and of his first meeting with Audouin in the primeval woods of Geauga County. He was flattered that Gwen should have asked him indirectly for his history: more flattered still to find that she listened to his hasty reminiscences with evident attention. He told her briefly about his early attempts at drawing in the blackberry bottom; how the deacon had regarded his artistic impulses as so many proofs of original sin; how he had followed the trappers out into the frozen woodland; how he had met Audouin there by accident; and how Audouin had praised his drawings and encouraged him in his fancies, being the first human being he had ever known who cared at all for any of these things. 'And when you spoke so kindly about my poor little landscape the other day, Miss Russell,' he added, looking down and hesitating, 'I felt more happy than I had ever felt before since that day so long ago, in the woods away over yonder in America.'

But Gwen only smiled back a frank smile of unaffected sympathy, and answered warmly, 'I'm so glad you think so much of my criticism, I'm sure, Mr. Winthrop.'

Then Hiram went on and told her how he had worked and struggled at school and college, and at the block-cutting establishment; and how he had longed to go to England and be an artist; and how he had never got the opportunity. And then he spoke of the first day he had ever seen Gwen herself by the Lake of the Thousand Islands.

Till that moment it hadn't struck Gwen how very earnest Hiram's voice was gradually growing; but as he came to that first chance meeting at Alexandria Bay, she couldn't help observing that his lips began to tremble a little, and that his words were thick with emotion. For a second she thought she ought to rise up and suggest that they should join the others over yonder in the garden: but then she changed her mind again, and felt sure she must be mistaken. The young American artist could never mean to have the boldness to propose to her on the strength of so little encouragement. And besides, his story was really so interesting, and she was so very anxious to hear out the rest of it to the very end.

'And so you liked England immensely?' she asked him, when he reached in due course that part of his simple straightforward confidences. 'I wonder you didn't stop there and take regularly to landscape painting.'

'I was sorely tempted to stop,' Hiram answered, daring to look her straight in the eyes now; for he almost flattered himself she knew what he was going to say to her next.

'I came away from England most reluctantly, at Mr. Audouin's particular request: but I longed at the time to remain, for I had borne two words ringing in my ears from America to England, and those two words were just two names—Gwen and Chester.'

Gwen started away suddenly with a half-frightened expression, and said to him in a colder tone, 'Why, what do you mean? Explain yourself, please, Mr. Winthrop. My name you know is Gwen, and papa and I used once to live in Chester.'

Hiram took her hand timidly in his with an air of gentle command, and made her sit down again once more for a minute upon the seat in the arbour. 'You must hear me out to the end now, Miss Bussell,' he said in a very soft, firm voice, 'whatever comes of it. You mustn't go away yet. I didn't mean to speak so soon, but I have been hurried into it. I've staked my whole existence on a single throw, and you mustn't run away and leave me in the midst of it undecided.'

Gwen turned pale with nervousness, and withdrew her hand, but sat quite still, and listened to him attentively.

'From the first moment I ever saw you, Miss Russell,' he went on passionately, 'I felt you were the only woman I had ever loved or ever could love. I didn't know your full name, or who you were, or where you lived; but I heard your father call you Gwen, and I heard you say you had been at Chester. Those were the only two things I knew at all about you. And from the day when I saw you there looking over my sketch beside the Thousand Islands, I kept those two names of Gwen and Chester engraved upon my heart until I came to Europe. I keep one of them engraved there still until this very minute. And whatever you say to me, I shall keep it there unaltered until I die.... Oh, Miss Russell, I don't want you to give me an answer at once, I hope you won't give me an answer at once, because I can see from your face what that answer would most likely be: but I love you, I love you, I love you; and as long as I live I shall always, always love you.'

'I think, Mr. Winthrop,' Gwen said, slowly rising and hesitating, 'we ought to go back now and join the others.'

Hiram looked at her with a concentrated look of terror and despair that fairly frightened her. 'Not for one moment

62

yet,' he whispered quite softly, 'not for one moment yet, I beg and pray of you. I have something else still to say to you.'

'*Not for one moment yet.*'

Original

Gwen faltered for another second, and then stood still and listened passively.

'Miss Russell,' he began again, with white lips and straining eyeballs, 'I don't want you to give me an answer yet; but I do want you to wait a little and consider with yourself before you give me it. If you say no to me all at once, you will kill me, you will kill me. I have lived for so many weary years in this hope, so long deferred, that it has become a part, as it were, of my very being, and you can't tear it out of me now without lacerating and rending me.

But I thought—I fancied—it was wildly presumptuous of me, but still I fancied—that this last week or two you had been more kind to me, more interested in me, more tolerant of me at least, than you used to be formerly.'

Gwen's heart smote her with genuine remorse when she heard that true accusation. Poor young fellow! She had undoubtedly led him into it, and she felt thoroughly ashamed of herself for the cruel ruse she had unwittingly practised upon him. Who would ever have thought, though, that the Yankee painter was really and truly so much in love with her?

She sighed slightly; for no woman can hear a man declare his heartfelt admiration for herself without emotion; and then she answered feebly, 'I... I... I only said I admired your pictures immensely, Mr. Winthrop.' Hiram could hardly gasp out a few words more. 'Oh, Miss Russell, don't give me an answer yet, don't give me an answer yet, I implore you. Wait and think it over a little while, and then answer me. You have never thought of me before in this way, I can see; you haven't any idea about me: wait and think it over, and remember that my whole life and happiness hangs upon it. Wait, oh! please wait and think it over.'

He pleaded with so much earnestness in his tone, and he looked so eagerly into her swimming eyes, that Gwen forgot for the moment his Yankee accent and his plain face and his unpolished manners, and saw him only as he was, an eager lover, begging her for mercy with all the restrained energy of a deep and self-contained but innately passionate nature. She could not help but pity him, he was so thoroughly and profoundly in earnest. For a moment her heart was really touched, not with love, but with infinite compassion, and she answered, half remorsefully, 'I'm afraid I can't hold you out much hope, Mr. Winthrop; but it shall be as you say; I will think it over, and let you have my full answer hereafter.' Hiram seized her hand eagerly. She tried to withdraw it, but he would not let her. 'Thank you,' he cried almost joyously; 'thank you, thank you! Then you don't refuse me utterly; you don't reject me without appeal; you will take my plea into consideration? I will not ask you again. I will not obtrude myself upon your notice unwillingly; but let me know in a fortnight. Do take a fortnight; my whole life is staked upon it; let it have a fortnight.'

Gwen's eyes were brimmed with two rising tears as she answered, trembling, 'Very well, it shall be a fortnight. Now we must go, Mr. Winthrop. We've stopped here too long. The others will be waiting for us.' And she drew her hand away from his as quietly as she was able, but not without a certain small inobtrusive sympathetic pressure. In her heart she pitied him.

As she passed out and joined the party at the far end of the garden, Hiram noticed that she didn't go up to speak at once to Colin Churchill. She let Audouin, nothing loth, lead her off down the alley of orange trees, and there she began speaking to him as if quite casually about Hiram.

'Your friend Mr. Winthrop has been telling me how kind you've been to him, and how much he owes to you,' she said, twirling a flower nervously between her fingers. 'How good of you to do all that you have done for him! Do you know, I quite envy you your opportunities for discovering such a genius in neglected places. I didn't know before, Mr. Audouin, that among all your other good qualities you were also a philanthropist. But your *protégé* there is quite warm and enthusiastic about all your goodness and kindness to him both here and in America.'

She looked straight at him all unconsciously as she spoke, and her eyes, though of course she had hastily wiped them on leaving the arbour, glistened a little still with the two tears that had risen unbidden to their lids when she was talking a minute before with Hiram. Audouin noticed the glistening with a quiet delight, and naturally coupled that and her words together into a mistaken meaning. 'If only we were quite alone now,' he thought to himself regretfully, 'this would be the exact moment to say what I wish to her. But no matter; another opportunity will crop up before long, I don't doubt, and then I can speak to her quite at my leisure.'

As for Gwen, when she found herself alone in her room that evening, she sat down in the easy-chair by the bedside, and took a most unconscionable time in unfastening her necklet and earrings, and putting them away one by one in the little jewel-case. 'He's very much in love with me, that's certain,' she said to herself meditatively. 'Who could ever have imagined it? I never should have talked to him so much if I had fancied he could possibly have misunderstood me. Poor fellow, I'm awfully sorry for him. And how dreadfully distressed he looked when I didn't answer him! It quite made me take a sort of fancy to him for the moment.... What a romantic history, too! Fell in love with me at first sight, that day by the Thousand Islands! And I never even so much as looked at him..... This necklet doesn't at all become me. I shall get another one next time I go down the Corso.... But he paints beautifully, and no doubt about it; and that charming Mr. Audouin says he's really quite an artistic genius. I'm positively grieved with myself that I shall have to refuse him. He'll break his heart over it, poor young man; I'm sure he'll break his heart over it. Of course one doesn't mind breaking most men's hearts one bit, because, you see, in the long run they're none the worse for it. But this young Mr. Winthrop's another sort of person; if you break his heart, just this one time only, that'll be the end of him at once and for ever.... And what an unhappy life he seems to have had of it, too! One would be quite sorry to

66

add to it by making him miserable with a refusal..... Ah, well, he's really a very good sort of young man in his way. What a pity he should be an American!... And yet why should Americans differ so much from other people, I wonder? What a wistful look he gave me when he asked me not to answer him now immediately. Upon my word, in a sort of way I really do like him just a little bit, the poor young fellow.'

CHAPTER XXXVI. CECCA SHOWS HER HAND.

H ave you brought me the medicine, Beppo?'

'The what, Signora Cecca? Oh, the medicine? I don't call it medicine: I call it — — — —'

Cecca clapped her hand angrily upon his lips. 'Fool,' she said, 'what are you babbling about? Give me the bottle and say no more about it. That's a good friend indeed. I owe you a thank-you for this, truly.'

'But, Cecca, what do you want it for? You must swear to me solemnly what you want it for. The police, you know — —'

Cecca laughed merrily—a joyous laugh, with no sorcery in it. One would have said, the guileless merriment of a little simple country maiden. 'The police, indeed,' she cried, softly but gaily. 'What have the police got to do with it, I wonder? I want to poison a cat, a monster of a cat, that wails and screams every night outside my window; and you must go and wrap the thing up in as much mystery as if— — Well, there! it's lucky nobody at Rome can understand good sound Calabrian even if they overhear it, or you'd go and make the folks suspicious with your silly talking—and so loud, too.'

Giuseppe looked at her, and muttered slowly something inarticulate. Then he looked again in a stealthy, frightened fashion; and at last he made up his mind to speak out boldly.

'Cecca! stop! I know what you want that little phial for.'

Cecca turned and smiled at him saucily. 'Oh, you know!' she said in a light ironical tone. 'You know, do you? Then, body of God, it's no use my telling you, so that's all about it.'

'Cecca,' the young man said again, snatching at the tiny bottle, which she still held gingerly between her finger and thumb, as if toying with it and fondling it, 'I've been watching you round at the Englishman's studio, and I've found out what you want the—the medicine for.'

Cecca's forehead puckered up quickly into a scowling frown (as when she sat for Clytemnestra), and she answered angrily, 'You've been playing the spy, then, have you really? I thank you, Signor Giuseppe, I thank you.'

'Listen, Cecca. I have been watching the Englishman's studio. There comes an English lady there, a beautiful tall lady, with a military father—a lady like this:' and Giuseppe put on in a moment a ludicrous caricature of Gwen's gait and carriage and manner. 'You have seen her, and you are jealous of her.'

Quick as lightning, Cecca saw her opportunity, and caught at it instinctively with Italian cunning. Giuseppe was right in principle, there was no denying it; but he had mistaken between Gwen and Minna. He had got upon the wrong tack, and she would not undeceive him. Keeping her forehead still dexterously bent to the same terrible scowl as before, and never for a second betraying her malicious internal smile of triumph, she answered, as if angry at being detected, 'Jealous! and of her! Signor Giuseppe, you are joking.'

'I am not joking, Cecca. I can see you are jealous this very moment. You love the Englishman. What is the good of loving him? He will not marry you, and you will not marry him: you would do much better to take, after all, to poor old Beppo. But you're jealous of the tall lady, because you think the Englishman's in love with her. What does it matter to you or me whether he is or whether he isn't? And it is for her that you want the medicine.'

Cecca drew a long breath and pretended to be completely baffled. 'Give me the bottle,' she cried; 'give me the bottle, Beppo.'

Giuseppe held it triumphantly at arm's length above his head.

'Not till you swear to me, Cecca, that you don't want to use it against the tall lady.' Cecca wrung her hands in mock despair. 'You won't give it to me, Beppo? You won't give it to me? What do you want me to swear it by? The holy water — the rosary — the medal of the holy father?'

Giuseppe smiled a smile of contemptuous superciliousness.

'Holy water! — rosary! — Pope!' he cried, 'Much you care for them indeed, Signora. No, no; you must swear by something that will bind you firmly. You must swear on your own little pocket image of Madonna della Guardia of Monteleone.'

Cecca pouted. (To the daughter of ten generations of Calabrian brigands a detail like a little poisoning case was merely a matter for careless pouting and feminine vagaries.)

'You will compel me?' she asked hesitatingly.

Giuseppe nodded.

'Or else I don't give you the bottle,' he murmured.

Cecca drew the little silver image with well-simulated reluctance from inside her plaited bodice. 'What am I to swear?' she asked petulantly.

'Say the words after me,' Beppo insisted. 'I swear by the mother of God, Madonna della Guardia of Monteleone, and all holy saints, that I will not touch or hurt or harm the tall English lady with the military father. And if I do may the Madonna forget me.'

Cecca repeated the words after him, severally and

70

distinctly. It was very necessary that she should be quite precise, lest the Madonna should by inadvertence make any mistake about the particular person. If she didn't make it quite clear at first that the oath only regarded Gwen, the Madonna might possibly be very angry with her for poisoning Minna, and that of course would be extremely awkward. It's a particularly unpleasant thing for any one to incur the displeasure of such a powerful lady as Madonna della Guardia at Monteleone.

'You may have the bottle now if you like,' Beppo said, handing it back to her carelessly.

Cecca pouted once more. 'What's the use of it now?' she asked languidly. 'Except, of course, to poison the cat with!'

Beppo laughed. To the simple unsophisticated Calabrian mind the whole episode only figured itself as a little bit of Cecca's pardonable feminine jealousy. Women will be women, and if they see a rival, of course, they'll naturally try to poison her. To say the truth, Beppo thought the fancy pretty and piquant on Cecca's part rather than otherwise. The fear of the Roman police was to him the only serious impediment.

'I may come and see you again next Sunday, Cecca?' he asked as he took up his bundle to leave the room. 'You owe me a little courtesy for this.'

Cecca smiled and nodded in a very gay humour. There was no need for deception now she had got the precious bottle securely put away in the innermost pocket of her model's kirtle. 'Yes,' she answered benignly. 'you may come on Sunday. You have deserved well of me.'

But as soon as Beppo had left the room Signora Cecca flung herself down upon the horsehair mattress in the corner (regardless of her back hair), and rolled over and over in her wild delight, and threw her arms about, as if she were posing for the Pythoness, and laughed aloud in her effusive southern joy and satisfaction. 'Ha! ha!' she cried to herself gaily, 'he thought it was that one! He thought it was that one, did he? He's got mighty particular since he came to Rome, Beppo has—afraid of the police, the coward; and he won't have anything to do even with poisoning a poor heretic of an Englishwoman. Madonna della Guardia, I have no such scruples for my part! But he mistook the one: he thought I was angry with the tall handsome one. No, no, she may do as she likes for all I care for her. It's the ugly little governess with the watery eyes that my Englishman's in love with. What he can see to admire in her I can't imagine—a thing with no figure—but he's in love with her, and she shall pay for it, the caitiff creature; she shall pay for it, I promise her. Here's the bottle, dear little bottle! How bright and clear it dances! Cecca Bianchelli, you shall have your revenge yet. Madonna della Guardia, good little Madonna, sweet little Madonna, you shall have your candles. Don't be angry with me, I pray you, Madonna mia, I shall not break my oath; it's the other one, the little governess, dear Madonna! She's only a heretic—an Englishwoman—a heretic; an affair of love, what would you have, Madonna? You shall get your candles, see if you don't, and your masses too, your two nice little masses, in your own pretty sweet little chapel on the high hill at Monteleone!'

CHAPTER XXXVII. CECCA AND MINNA.

It was Tuesday afternoon at Colin Churchill's, and Minna had got her usual weekly leave to go and visit her cousin at his own studio. 'I find her devotion admirable,' said Madame, 'but then, this cousin he is young and handsome. After all, there is perhaps nothing so very extraordinary in it, really.'

Cecca was there, too, waiting her opportunity, with the little phial always in her pocket: for who knows when Madonna della Guardia may see the chance of earning her two promised masses? She is late this afternoon, the English governess; but she will come soon: she never forgets to come every Tuesday.

By and by, Minna duly arrived, and Colin kissed her before Cecca's very eyes—the miscreant! and she took off her bonnet even, and sat down and seemed quite prepared to make an afternoon of it.

'Cecca,' Colin cried, 'will you ask them to make us three cups of coffee?—You can stop, Minna, and have some coffee, can't you?'

Cecca didn't understand the English half of the sentence, of course, but she ran off quite enchanted to execute the little commission in the Italian bent of it. A cup of coffee! It was the very thing; Madonna della Guardia, what fortune you have sent me!

Colin and Minna sat talking within while the coffee was brewing, and when it was brought in, Cecca waited for her opportunity cautiously, until Minna had taken a cup for herself, and laid it down upon the little bare wooden table

74

beside her. It would never do to put the medicine by mistake into the cup of the Englishman; we must manage these little matters with all due care and circumspection. So Cecca watched in the background, as a cat watches a mouse's hole with the greatest silence and diligence, till at last a favourable chance occurred: and then under the pretence of handing Minna the biscuits which came up with the coffee, she managed cleverly to drop half the contents of the phial into the cup beside her. Half was quite enough for one trial: she kept the other half, in case of accident, to use again if circumstances should demand it.

Just at that moment a note came in from Maragliano. Could Colin step round to the other studio for a quarter of an hour? A wealthy patron had dropped in, and wanted to consult with him there about a commission.

Cohn read the letter through hastily; explained its contents to Minna; kissed her once more: (Ha, the last time, the last time for ever! he will never do that again, the Englishman!) and then ran out to see the wealthy patron.

Minna was left alone for that half-hour in the studio with Cecca.

Would she drink the coffee, now? that was the question. No, as bad luck and all the devils would have it, she didn't seem to think of tasting or sipping it. A thousand maledictions! The stuff would get cold, and then she would throw it away and ask for another cupful. Blessed Madonna of Monte-leone, make her drink it! Make her drink it! Bethink you, unless she does, dear little Madonna, you do not get your candles or your masses!

Still Minna sat quite silent and motionless, looking vacantly at the beautiful model, whom she had forgotten now to feel angry or jealous about. She was thinking, thinking vacantly; and her Italian was so far from fluent that she didn't feel inclined to begin a conversation off-hand

75

with the beautiful model.

Just to encourage her, then (there's nothing like society), Ceeca drew up her three-legged stool close beside the signorina, and began to sip carelessly and unconcernedly at her own cup of coffee. Perhaps the sight of somebody else drinking might chance by good luck to make the Englishwoman feel a little thirsty.

But Minna only looked at her, and smiled half-unconsciously. To her great surprise, the Italian woman perceived that two tears were slowly trickling down her rival's cheeks.

Italians are naturally sympathetic, even when they are on the eve of poisoning you; and besides one is always curious to know what one is crying for. So Cecca leaned forward kindly, and said in her gentlest tone: 'You are distressed, signorina. You are suffering in some way. Can I do anything for you?'

Minna started, and wiped away the two tears hastily. 'It is nothing,' she said, 'I didn't mean it. I—I fancied I was alone, I had forgotten.'

'What! you speak Italian!' Cecca cried, a little astonished, and half anxious to enjoy her triumph by anticipation. 'Ah, signorina, I know what is the matter. I have guessed your secret: I have guessed your secret!'

Minna blushed. 'Hush,' she said eagerly. 'Not a word about it. My friend may return. Not a word about it.'

But still she didn't touch her coffee.

Then Cecca began to talk to her gently and soothingly, in her best soft Italian manner. Poor thing, she was evidently very sad. So far away from her home too. Cecca was really quite sorry for her. She tried to draw her out and in her way to comfort her. The signorina hadn't long to live: let us at least be kind and sympathetic to her.

For, you see, an Italian woman is capable of poisoning you in such a perfectly good-humoured and almost affectionate fashion.

At first, Minna didn't warm very much to the beautiful model: she had still her innate horror of Italian women strong upon her; and besides she knew from her first meeting that Cecca had a terrible vindictive temper. But in time Cecca managed to engage her in real conversation, and to tell her about her own little personal peasant history. Yes, Cecca came from Calabria, from that beautiful province; and her father, her father was a fisherman.

Minna started. 'A fisherman! How strange. And my father too, was also a fisherman away over yonder in England!'

It was Cecca's turn to start at that. A fisherman! How extraordinary. She could hardly believe it. She took it for granted all along that Minna, though a governess, was a grand English lady; for the idea of a fisher man's daughter dressing and living in the way that Minna did was almost inconceivable to the unsophisticated mind of a Calabrian peasant woman. And to wear a bonnet, too! to wear a bonnet!

'Tell me all about it,' Cecca said, drawing closer, and genuinely interested (with a side eye upon the untasted coffee). 'You came to Rome then,' jerking her two hands in the direction of the door, 'to follow the Englishman?' 'Signora Cecca,' Minna said, with a sudden vague instinct, in her tentative Italian, 'I will trust you. I will tell you all about it. I was a poor fisherman's daughter in England, and I always loved my cousin, the sculptor.' Cecca listened with the intensest interest. Minna lifted her cup for the first time, and took a single sip of the poisoned coffee.

'Good!' thought Cecca calmly to herself. 'If she takes a first sip, why of course in that case she will certainly finish it.'

Then Minna went on with her story, shortly and in

difficulty, pieced out every here and there by Cecca's questions and ready pantomime. Cecca drank in all the story with the deepest avidity. It was so strange that something should just then have moved the Englishwoman to make a *confidante* of her. A poor fisherman's daughter, and neglected now by her lover who had become a grand and wealthy sculptor! Mother of God, from the bottom of her heart, she really pitied her.

'And when he came to Rome,' Cecca said, helping out the story of her own accord, 'he fell in with the grand English ladies like the one with the military papa; and they made much of him; and you were afraid, my little signorina, that he had almost forgotten you! And so you came to Rome on purpose to follow him.'

Minna nodded, and her eyes filled with tears a second time.

'Poor little signorina!' Cecca said earnestly.

'It was cruel of him, very cruel of him. But when people come to Rome they are often cruel, and they soon forget their lovers of the province.' Something within her made her think that moment of poor Giuseppe, who had followed her so trustfully from that far Calabria.

Minna raised the cup once more, and took another sip at the poisoned coffee. Cecca watched the action closely, and this time gave a small involuntary sigh of relief when Minna set it down again almost untasted. Poor little thing! after all she was only a fisherman's daughter, and she wanted her lover, her lover of the province, to love her still the same as ever! Nothing so very wrong or surprising in that! Natural, most natural.... But then, the Englishman, the Englishman! she mustn't be allowed to carry off the Englishman.... And Giuseppe, poor Giuseppe.... Well, there, you know; in love and war these things will happen, and one can't avoid them.

'And you knew him from a child?' she asked innocently.

78

'Yes, from a child. We lived together in a little village by the sea-shore in England; my father was a fisherman, and his a gardener. He used to go into the fields by the village, and make me little images of mud, which I used to keep upon my mantelpiece, and that was the first beginning, you see, of his sculpture.'

Mother of heaven, just like herself and Giuseppe! How they used to play together as children on the long straight shore at Monteleone. 'But you were not Christians in England, you were pagans, not Christians!'

For the idea of images had suggested to Cecca's naïve mind the notion of the Madonna.

Minna almost laughed, in spite of herself, at the curious misapprehension, and drew out from her bosom the little cross that she always wore instead of a locket. 'Oh yes,' she said simply, without dwelling upon any minor points of difference between them; 'we are Christians—Christians.'

The girl examined the cross reverently, and then looked back at the coffee with a momentary misgiving. After all, the Englishwoman was very gentle and human-like and kind-hearted. It was natural she should want to keep her country lover. And besides she was really, it seemed, no heretic in the end at all, but a good Christian.

'When people come to Rome and become famous,' she repeated musingly, 'they do wrong to be proud and to forget the lovers of their childhood.' Giuseppe loved her dearly, there was no denying it, and she used to love him dearly, too, down yonder on the shore at Monteleone.

Minna raised her cup of coffee a third time, and took a deeper drink. Nearly a quarter of the whole was gone now; but not much of the poison, Cecca thought to herself, thank heaven; that was heavy and must have sunk to the bottom. If only one could change the cups now, without being observed! Poor little thing, it would be a pity, certainly, to

79

poison her. One oughtn't to poison people, properly speaking, unless one has really got some serious grudge against them. She was a good little soul, though no doubt insipid, and a Christian, too; Madonna della Guardia, would the bargain hold good, Cecca wondered silently, seeing the Englishwoman had miraculously turned out to be after all a veritable Christian. These are points of casuistry on which one would certainly like to have beforehand the sound opinion of a good unprejudiced Calabrian confessor.

'You think he makes too much of the tall signorina!' Cecca said lightly, smiling and nodding. (Cecca had, of course, an immense fund of sympathy with the emotion of jealousy in other women.)

Minna blushed and looked down timidly without answering. What on earth could have possessed her to make so free, at this particular minute, with this terrible Italian model woman? She really couldn't make it out herself, and yet she knew there had been some strange unwonted impulse moving within her. (If she had read Von Hartmann, she would have called it learnedly the action of the Unconscious. As it was, she would have said, if she had known all, that it was a Special Providence.)

So wishing merely to change the subject, and having nothing else to say at the moment, she looked up almost accidentally at the completed clay of the Nymph Bathing, and said simply: 'That is a beautiful statue, Signora Cecca.'

Cecca smiled a majestic smile of womanly gratification, and showed her double row of even regular pearl-white teeth with coquettish beauty. 'I posed for it,' she said, throwing herself almost unconsciously into the familiar attitude. 'It is my portrait!'

'It is a splendid portrait,' Minna answered cordially, glancing quickly from the original to the copy, 'a splendid portrait of a very beautiful and exquisitely formed woman.'

'Signorina!' Cecca cried, standing up in front of her, and roused by a sudden outburst of spontaneous feeling to change her plan entirely, 'you are quite mistaken; the master does not love the tall lady. I know the master well, I have been here all the time, I have watched him narrowly. He does not love the tall lady: she loves him, I tell you, but he does not care for her; in his heart of hearts he does not love her; I know, for I have watched them. Signorina, I like you, you are a sweet little Englishwoman, and I like you dearly. Your friend from the village in England shall marry you!' ('Oh, don't talk so!' Minna cried parenthetically, hiding her face passionately between her hands.)

'And if the tall lady were to try to come between you and him,' Cecca added vigorously, 'I would poison her—I would poison her—I would poison her! She shall not steal another woman's lover, the wretched creature. I hate such meanness, signorina, I will poison her.'

As Cecca said those words, with an unfeigned air of the deepest and most benevolent sympathy, she managed to catch her long loose scarf as if by accident in the corner of the light table where Minna's half-finished cup of coffee was still standing, and to upset it carelessly on to the floor of the studio. The cup with a crash broke into a hundred pieces.

At that very moment Colin entered. He saw Minna rising hastily from the settee beside the overturned table, and Cecca down on her knees upon the floor, wiping up the coffee hurriedly with one of the coarse studio towels. Cecca looked up in his face with a fearless glance as if nothing unusual had happened. 'An accident, signor,' she cried: 'my scarf caught in the table. I have spilt the signorina's cup of coffee. But no matter. I will run down immediately and tell them below to make her another.'

'Cecca and I have been talking together, Colin,' Minna

said, replacing the fallen table hastily, 'and, do you know, isn't it strange, she's a fisherman's daughter in Calabria? and oh! Colin, I don't believe after all she's really half such a bad sort of girl as I took her to be when I first saw her. She's been talking to me here quite nicely and sympathetically.'

'Italians are all alike,' Colin answered, with the usual glib English faculty for generalisation about all 'foreigners.' 'They'll be ready to stab you one minute, and to fall upon your neck and kiss you the very next.'

Going out of the studio to order more coffee from the trattoria next door, Cecca happened to meet on the doorstep with her friend Giuseppe.

'Beppo,' she said, looking up at him more kindly than had been her wont of late: 'Beppo, I want to tell you something —I've changed my mind about our little difference. If you like, next Sunday you may marry me.'

'Next Sunday! Marry you!' Beppo exclaimed, astonished. 'Oh, Cecca, Cecca, you cannot mean it!'

'I said, next Sunday, if you like, you may marry me. That's good ordinary sensible Calabrian, isn't it? If you wish, I'll give it you in Tuscan: you can understand nothing but Tuscan, it seems, since you came to Rome, my little brother.'

She said the words tenderly, banter as they were, in their own native dialect: and Beppo saw at once that she was really in earnest.

'But next Sunday,' he exclaimed. 'Next Sunday, my little one! And the preparations?'

'I am rich!' Cecca answered calmly. 'I bring you a dower. I am the most favourite model in all Rome this very moment.'

'And the Englishman—the Englishman? What are you going to do with the Englishman?'

'The Englishman may marry his sweetheart if he will,' the

girl replied with dogged carelessness.

'Cecca! you did not give the.... medicine to the Englishman?'

Cecca drew the half-empty bottle from her pocket and dashed it savagely against the small paving-stones in the alley underfoot. 'There,' she cried, eagerly, as she watched it shiver into little fragments. 'See the medicine! That is the end of it.'

'And the cat, Cecca?'

Cecca drew a long breath. 'How much of it would hurt a human being—a woman?' she asked anxiously. 'Somebody has drunk a little by mistake—just so much!' And she measured the quantity approximately with the tip of her nail upon her little finger.

Giuseppe shook his head re-assuringly, shrugged his shoulders, and opened his hands, palms outward, as if to show he was evidently making no mental reservation. 'Harmless!' he said. Quite harmless. It would take a quarter of a phial at least to produce any effect worth speaking of.'

Cecca clasped her silver image of the Madonna ecstatically. 'That's well, Beppo,' she answered with a nod. 'I must go now. On Sunday, little brother! On Sunday. Beppo—Beppo —it was all a play. I love you. I love you.'

But as she went in to order the coffee the next second, she said to herself with a regretful grimace: 'What a fool I was after all to waste the medicine! Why, if only I had thought of it. I might have used it to poison the other one, the tall Englishwoman. She shall not be allowed to steal away the little signorina's lover!'

CHAPTER XXXVIII. GWEN HAS A VISITOR.

In the gardens of the Villa Panormi, Gwen Howard-Russell was walking up and down by herself one morning, a few days later, among the winter flowers (for it was now January), when she saw a figure she fancied she could recognise entering cautiously at the main gate by the high road to the Ponte Molle. Why, yes, she couldn't be mistaken. It was certainly the woman Cecca, the beautiful model down at Mr. Colin Churchill's studio! How very extraordinary and mysterious! What on earth could she be coming here for?

Gwen walked quickly down to meet the girl, who stood half hesitating in the big central avenue, and asked her curiously what she wanted.

'Signorina,' Cecca answered, not unrespectfully, 'I wish to speak with you a few minutes in private.'

Gwen was surprised and amused at this proposal, but not in the least disconcerted. How deliciously Italian and romantic! Mr. Churchill had sent her a letter, no doubt—perhaps a declaration—and he had employed the beautiful model to be the naturally appropriate bearer of it. There's something in the very air of Rome that somehow lends itself spontaneously to these delightful mystifications. In London, now, his letter would have been delivered in the ordinary course of business by the common postman! How much more poetical, and antique, and romantic, to send it round by the veritable hands of his own beautiful imaginary Wood Nymph!

'Come this way,' she said, in her imperious English fashion; 41 will speak with you down here in the bower.'

Cecca followed her to the bower in silence, for she resented our brusque insular manners: and somewhat to Gwen's surprise when she reached the bower, she seated herself like an equal upon the bench beside her. These Italians have no idea of the natural distinctions between the various social classes.

'Well,' Gwen asked, after a moment's pause. 'What do you want to say to me? Have you brought me any message or letter?'

'No, signorina,' the girl answered somewhat maliciously. 'Nothing: nothing. I come to speak to you of my own accord solely.'

There was another short pause, as though Cecca expected the English lady to make some further inquiry: but as Gwen said nothing, Cecca began again: 'I want to tell you something, signorina. You know the little English governess, the master's cousin?'

'Yes, I know her. That is to say, I have met her.'

'Well, I have come to tell you something about her. She is a fisherman's daughter, as I am, and she was brought up, far away, in a village in England, together with the master.'

'I know all about her,' Gwen answered somewhat coldly. 'She was a servant afterwards at a house in London, and then she became a teacher in a school, and finally a governess. I have heard all that before, from a friend of mine in England.'

'But I have something else to tell you about her,' Cecca continued with unusual self-restraint for an Italian woman. 'Something else that concerns you personally. She was brought up with the master, and she used to play with him in the meadows, when she was a child, where he made her little images of the Madonna in clay; and that was how he first of all began to be a sculptor. Then she followed him from her village to a city: and there he learned to be more of

86

a sculptor. By-and-by, he came to Rome: but still, the little signorina loved him and wished to follow him. And at last she did follow him, because she loved him. And the master loves her, too, and is very fond of her. That is all that I have to tell you.'

She kept her eye fixed steadily on Gwen while she spoke, and watched in her cat-like fashion to see whether the simple story was telling home, as she meant it to do, to Gwen's intelligence. As she uttered the words she saw Gwen's face grow suddenly scarlet, and she knew she had rightly effected her intended purpose. She had struck the right chord in Gwen's pride, and Minna now would have nothing more to fear from the tall Englishwoman. 'Safer than the poison,' she thought to herself reflectively, 'and as it happens, every bit as useful and effectual, without half the trouble or danger.'

Gwen looked at her steadily and without flinching. 'Why do you say all this to *me*?' she asked haughtily.

'Because I knew it closely concerned you,' Cecca replied, in her coolest tone: 'and I see from your face, too, signorina, whatever you choose to say, that I was not mistaken.'

And indeed, in that one moment, the whole truth about Minna and Colin, never before even suspected by her, had flashed suddenly across Gwen's mind with the most startling vividness. She saw it all now, as clear as daylight. How could she ever have been foolish enough for a moment not to have understood it? Colin Churchill didn't make love to her for the very best of all possible reasons, because he was already in love with another person: and that other person was nobody else but the little governess with the old-fashioned bonnet. She reeled a little at the suddenness of the revelation, but she managed somehow or other to master her confusion and even to assume externally a careless demeanour.

'But what interest have *you* in telling me this?' she asked again of Cecca haughtily.

'Because I like the little signorina,' Cecca answered quite truthfully, 'and I was anxious to do anything on earth I could to serve her.'

After all, except for her casual little provincial leaning towards the use of poison (quite pardonable in a pretty Calabrian), Cecca was really not a bad sort of girl at bottom, as girls go in this strange and oddly blended universe of ours.

'Is that all you have to say to me?' Gwen enquired after another short pause, with ill-affected languor, of the beautiful model.

'That is all, signorina. I see you understand me. Good morning.'

'Stop!' Gwen said, taking out her purse uneasily. 'You have done me, too, a service, my girl. Take that for your trouble in coming here.'

Cecca drew herself up proudly to her full height. She was an Italian peasant woman, and yet she could resist an offer of money. 'No, no, signorina,' she answered as haughtily as Gwen herself. 'I want no reward: I am rich, I am the queen of the models. I did it for love of the little lady.' And she walked with a stately salute out of the bower and down the solid marble steps of the great garden.

When she was gone, Gwen buried her face in her hands for a moment, and cried bitterly. It was not so much the disappointment that she felt, though she had really been very much in love with Colin Churchill, as the humiliation of knowing that Cecca had discovered both her secret and her disappointment. And indeed, Cecca's short disclosure had given a sudden death-blow to all Gwen's dearest and most deeply-rooted projects. In the inmost depths of her proud heart, Gwen Howard-Russell felt with instinctive unquestioning resolution that it would be impossible now under any circumstances for her to marry Colin Churchill. If it had been any other woman in the world save only little simple Minna, Gwen might have taken a sort of keen delight of battle in winning her sweetheart's love cleverly away from her. She might have fought her for her lover all along the line with feminine strategy, and enjoyed the victory all the better in the end because she had had to struggle hard for it. For though our hypocritical varnished civilisation is loth to confess it, in Europe at least it is always the women who are competing covertly among themselves for the small possible stock of husbands. How can it be otherwise when for every 'eligible' man in our society there are usually about half a dozen marriageable women? But the moment Gwen knew and realised that Colin was in love with Minna, or even that Minna was in love with Colin, she felt immediately that the game was now rendered absolutely impossible; for Minna had once been a servant, a common servant, a London parlour-maid, and Gwen Howard-Bussell could not for one moment bring down her proud head to treat a servant as even a conceivable rival. Oh, no, as soon as she thought it possible that Minna might even in her own heart aspire to marry Colin Churchill, there was nothing on earth left for her but to retire immediately from the utterly untenable position.

She could have married Colin himself, of course, in spite of all his past, as humble even as Minna's, for he had genius; and in a man genius is universally allowed to atone for everything. A woman may stoop to marry a man below her own position in the social scale by birth, if it is generally understood that she does it as a graceful and appreciative tribute to literary, scientific, or artistic greatness. But to put herself in rivalry as it were with a woman, not even a genius, and born beneath her, in a struggle for the hand of such a man, who ought rather of course to receive hers gratefully, as a distinguished favour—why, the whole thing is obviously an absolute impossibility. So Gwen dried her eyes as well as she was able, with her little dainty cambric pocket-handkerchief, and settled with herself at once and finally that the Colin Churchill day-dream was now at last dispelled for ever.

He was in love with the little governess—the little governess with the old-fashioned bonnet! And the little governess had been a parlour-maid in London! And she herself, Gwen Howard-Russell, had been on the very verge of putting herself in unworthy rivalry with her! She shuddered to think of it, actually shuddered even to think of it. The very idea was so horribly repugnant to her. And how many women of her own social status are there in this realm of England who would not have sympathised therein with Gwen Howard-Russell? Our pride is so much stronger than our Christianity, and in this case, oddly enough, the one power brought about pretty much the same practical result in the long run as the other.

As Gwen rose with red eyes and flushed cheeks, to make her way back to her own bedroom, she saw, as she passed along the shrubby orache hedge that separated the garden from the high-road, a wistful face looking anxiously and eagerly from outside, in the direction of the great villa. She knew in a moment whose it was: it was Hiram Winthrop's. He had stolen away from his studio and the Capture of Babylon, to come out that morning to the dusty roads of the suburbs, and see if he could catch a passing glimpse anywhere of Gwen Howard-Russell. His face was pale and anxious, and Gwen saw for herself in a second that he was wasted with his eagerness in waiting for her deferred answer. Her heart went forth for the moment to that sad devoted expression. 'Poor fellow,' she muttered to herself compassionately, 4 he's very much in love with me, very much in love with me. I wish to goodness I could only have given him a favourable answer.'

CHAPTER XXXIX. GWEN'S DECISION.

There were five days yet to run before the expiration of the fortnight which Gwen had promised to give to the consideration of Hiram's proposal, and in the course of those five days Gwen met her Yankee admirer again, quite accidentally, on two separate occasions, though both times in company with other people. Half insensibly to herself, since the sudden collapse of that little bubble fancy about Colin Churchill, she had begun to take a somewhat different view of poor Hiram's earnest entreaty. Of course she didn't in the least intend to say *yes* to him at last, in spite of Cecca's timely disclosures; she wasn't the sort of girl to go and throw herself into the arms of the very first man who happened to ask her, for no better reason in the world than merely because she had just met with a first serious disappointment; but still, she couldn't help reflecting to herself how deeply the young American was in love with her, and contrasting his eager, single-hearted, childlike devotion with the English sculptor's utter insensibility and curious indifference. Ah, yes, there could be no denying that much at any rate, that Hiram Winthrop was most profoundly and desperately in love with her. Love at first sight, too! How very romantic! He had carried away her image for ever with him through all these long weary years, ever since the day when he first met her, so long ago, by the merest accident, beside the Lake of the Thousand Islands.

A first serious disappointment, did she say? Well, well, that was really making a great deal too much, even to herself, of a girl's mere passing maidenly fancy. She had never herself been actually in love—not to say exactly *in love*, you know—with Mr. Colin Churchill. Oh, no, she had never gone so far as that, of course, even in her most unguarded moments of self-abandoned day-dreaming. Girls will have their fancies, naturally, and one can't prevent them; you think a particular young man is rather nice, and rather handsome, and rather agreeable; and you imagine to yourself that if he were to pay you any very marked attentions, don't you know—well there, one can't help having one's little personal preferences, anyhow, now can one? But as to saying she was ever really *in love* with Mr. Churchill—why, how can you possibly ever be in love with a man who never for a single moment takes as much as the slightest notice of you? And yet—how odd!—men and women must certainly be very differently constituted in these respects, when one comes to think of it; for that poor little Mr. Winthrop had been madly in love with her for years and years, almost without her ever even so much as for one moment discovering it or suspecting it!

Oh, no, she had never been in the least *in love* with Mr. Colin Churchill. And even if she had been (which she hadn't, but only—well, what you may call rather struck with him, he was such a very clever sculptor, and she was always so fond of artists' society)—but still, even if she had been (just to put the case, you know), she couldn't think of going on with it any further now, of course, for it wouldn't be Christian to try and entice that poor little governess girl's lover away from her, even if it hadn't been the case that she had been once upon a time a common servant. Poor little thing! though it was a pity that Mr. Churchill should ever think of throwing himself away on such an utter little nonentity as she was, still it would be very hard on her undoubtedly, if, after she had taken the trouble to raise herself as much as she could into his position in life, she should go and lose her lover after all, that she had so long been looking up to. Yes, in its own way it was a very proper arrangement indeed that Mr. Churchill should end at last by marrying the poor little dowdy governess.

And yet he was a very great sculptor, to be sure, and she, Gwen, had always had a wonderful fancy for marrying an artist.

But Mr. Winthrop's landscapes were really very beautiful too; and after all, painters are so very much more human in the end than those cold, impassive, marble-hearted sculptors. And what a lonely life Mr. Winthrop had always led! and how he seemed to yearn and hunger and thirst, as he spoke to her, for warm living and human sympathy! He had never had a sister, he said, and his mother, crushed and wearied by hard farm life and his father's religious sternness, had died while he was still a mere schoolboy. And he had never known anybody he could love but Gwen, except only, of course, dear Mr. Audouin; and after all, say what you will of it, a man, you know, a man is not a woman. Poor fellow, in her heart of hearts she was really sorry for him. And what a rage papa would be in, too, if only she were to accept him!

Papa would certainly be in a most dreadful temper; that was really quite undeniable. Gwen hardly knew herself, in fact, what ever he would do or say to her. He had a most unreasoning objection to artists in the concrete, regarding them, in fact, as scarcely respectable, and he had a still more unreasoning objection to all Americans, whom he hated, root and branch, as a set of vulgar, obtrusive, upstart nobodies. To be sure, Mr. Winthrop, now, was by no means obtrusive: quite the contrary; nor was he even vulgar, though he *did* certainly speak with a very faint American accent; and as to his being a nobody, why, if it came to that, of course it was papa himself who was really the nobody (though he *was* a Howard-Russell and a colonel in the line), while Mr. Winthrop was a very clever and interesting artist. So in fact, if, —just to put the case again—she ever *did* decide upon accepting him, she wasn't going to stand any nonsense of that sort from papa, you know, and that was just the long and the short of it.

With a girl of Gwen's high-spirited temperament it is probable that Hiram could hardly have had a better ally in his somewhat hopeless suit than this dim hypothetical consciousness on her part of the colonel's decided objection to Hiram as a possible husband.

If you want very much to marry a girl like Gwen, suggest to her incidentally, as you make your offer, that her parents will of course be very much opposed to a marriage between you. If that doesn't decide her to take your view of the matter, nothing on earth will, you may depend upon it.

And so the fortnight sped away, and at the end of it, Hiram Winthrop came up, as if by accident, one morning early to the Villa Panormi. The earl and the colonel were having a quiet game, with their after-breakfast cigars, in the billiard-room, and Hiram and Gwen had the big salon entirely to themselves for their final interview.

As Hiram entered, hardly daring to hope, and pale with restrained passion, Gwen had already made up her mind beforehand that she must say no to him: but at the very sight of his earnest face and worn eyelids her resolution suddenly faltered. He was desperately in love with her:— that was certain; she could hardly find it in her heart to dismiss him summarily. She would delay and temporise with him just for the moment. Poor fellow, if she blurted it out to him too bluntly and hastily, it might almost stun him. She would break her refusal to him gently, very gently.

'Well, Miss Russell,' he said to her eagerly, taking her hand as he entered with a faint hesitating pressure, 'you see I have come back for my answer; but before you give it to me, for good or for evil, there are one or two matters yet that I want to talk over with you very particularly.'

Gwen trembled a little as she seated herself on the big centre ottoman, and answered nervously, 'Well, Mr. Winthrop, then let me hear them.'

'I ought to plead for myself,' Hiram went on in a feverish voice, looking down on the ground and then up in her face alternately every half second. 'I ought to plead for myself with all my power, and all my soul, and all my energy, Miss Russell; for though to you this is only a matter of saying yes or no to one more suitor—and no doubt you have had many—to me it is a matter of life and death, for I never in my life for one moment imagined that I loved or could love any other woman; and if you refuse me now, I never in my life shall love another. If you refuse me, I shall lose heart altogether, and throw up this foolish painting business at once and for ever, and go back again to drive the plough and cut the corn once more in my own country. To that I have made my mind up irrevocably; so I ought to plead for myself, seeing how much is at stake, with all my heart and soul and energy.'

Gwen crumpled up the corners of the oriental antimacassar in her tremulous fingers as she answered very softly, 'I should be sorry to think you meant to do anything so unwise and so unjust to the world and to yourself on my account, Mr. Winthrop.'

'I ought to plead for myself, and to plead only,' Hiram went on, like one who has got a message to deliver and feels impelled to deliver it without heed of interruptions. 'I ought to say nothing that might in any way interfere with any faint chance I may possibly possess of winning your favour. I know how little likely I am to succeed, and I can't bear to make my own case seem still weaker and feebler to you. But, Miss Russell, before you answer me—and I'm not going to let you answer me yet, until you have heard me to the end fully—there are one or two things more I feel constrained to

96

say to you. I want to make you understand exactly what you will have to do and to put up with if by any chance you promise to marry me.' (Gwen blushed slightly at the word, so seriously spoken, but could not take her eyes away from his earnest face as he still went on rapidly speaking.) 'In the first place, I am a very poor painter, and I have nothing on earth but my art to live upon.'

'If that were all,' Gwen said, unconsciously taking his part, as it were, 'I don't think that to be an artist's wife, however poor he may be, is a life that any woman on earth need be anything but proud of.'

'Thank you,' Hiram said fervidly, looking up at her once more with a sudden gleam of newborn hope upon his pale worn countenance. 'Thank you, thank you. I know you are one of those who can value art at its true worth, and I was sure before I spoke that that at least need be no barrier between us. And as I am an American, and as proud of my old Puritan New England ancestry as any gentleman in old England could possibly be of his Norman forefathers or his broad acres, I won't pretend to apologise to you on the score of birth, or connections, or social position. That is a thing, if you will excuse my saying so, Miss Russell, that no American can under any circumstances stoop to do. Your father is proud, I know; but every descendant of the New England pilgrims is indeed in his own democratic way a great deal prouder.'

That was a point of view that, to say the truth, had never struck Gwen before as even possible; still, as Hiram said it, so boldly and unaffectedly, she felt in her heart that it was really nothing more than the truth, and though she couldn't quite understand it or sympathise with the feeling, she respected him for it, and admired his open manliness in saying it so straightforwardly.

'But while I think nothing of what your own relations

would doubtless consider the disparity in our positions,' Hiram went on earnestly, 'I do think a great deal of this—that I have at present absolutely no means of my own upon which to marry. If you consent, as I begin to hope you will consent, to be my wife, sooner or later, we may have to wait a long long time, perhaps even for years, before we can marry. I have risked everything upon my success as a painter. I have eaten up my capital to keep myself alive through my student period. I can find no purchasers now for the pictures I am painting. And I don't know whether the public will ever care to buy them at all, because I can't make up my own mind, even, whether I really am or am not a tolerable painter.'

'Upon that point, Mr. Winthrop,' Gwen said decidedly, 'I haven't myself the very slightest doubt or hesitation. I *know* you are a painter, and a very touching one; and I'm sure the world must find it out some day, sooner or later.'

Quite unconsciously to himself, Hiram was playing his own game in the very surest possible manner by seeming to take sides for the moment against himself, and so compelling Gwen, out of the mere necessities of the conversation, to argue the case for the defence with all a woman's momentary impetuosity.

'But I ought to have thought of all this before I ever spoke to you at all,' he went on earnestly. 'I ought to have reflected how cruel it was of me to ask you for a promise when I couldn't even tell whether I might ever be in a position to enable you to perform it. It was wrong of me, very wrong; and I felt angry with myself for having been led into doing it, the minute after I left you. But I was betrayed into my confession by the accidents of the moment. You must forgive me, because I had loved you so long—and so silently. I wouldn't have spoken to you even then if I hadn't imagined —it was ever so wrong and foolish of me, but still I imagined—that you seemed just then to be a little more interested than before in my work and my future. Oh, Miss Russell, I have loved you desperately; and I ventured, therefore, in a moment of haste to tell you that I loved you. But if you say *yes* to me to-day, it may be years and years, perhaps, before we can marry. I can't say when or how I may ever begin to earn my livelihood at all by painting pictures.'

'If I really loved a man, Mr. Winthrop,' Gwen answered in a lower voice, 'I shouldn't be afraid to wait for him as long as ever circumstances compelled it—if I really loved him. And apart altogether from that question, which you say I am not at present to answer, I can't believe that the world will be much longer yet in discovering that you have genius —yes, I *will* say genius. Mr. Churchill himself declares he is quite certain you have real genius.'

Hiram smiled and shook his head incredulously. 'Still,' he said, 'it is at least some comfort to me to know that, putting the matter in its most abstract form, you have no absolute objection to a long engagement. If you loved a man, you would be ready to wait for him. I knew you would, indeed, like every brave and true woman. I didn't doubt that you could be steadfast enough to wait; I only doubted whether it would be just of any man to beg you to wait under such more than doubtful circumstances. But, remember, Miss Russell, I have this excuse to plead in my own case, that it wasn't the passing fancy of a moment, but a love that has grown with me into my very being. There is only one more consideration now before I go on to ask you that final answer to my question, and it is this. You must reflect whether you would be willing to brave the anger of your father. I can't disguise from myself the fact that Colonel Howard-Russell would be very ill satisfied at the idea of your waiting to marry a penniless unknown American painter.'

Gwen looked at him proudly, almost defiantly, as she answered in a clear bold tone, 'If I loved a man really, Mr. Winthrop, I would marry him and wait for him as long as *I* chose, even if my father cast me off for it for ever the very next minute. If ever I marry I shall marry because I have consulted my own heart, and not because I have consulted my father.'

'I knew that too,' Hiram answered, with just a touch of triumph in his trembling voice. 'I only spoke to you about it because I thought it right to clear the ground entirely for my final question. Then, Gwen, Gwen, Gwen—I will call you Gwen for this once in my life, if I never call you Gwen again as long as I live here; I have thought of you as Gwen for all these years, and I will think of you so still, whatever comes, till my dying minute—oh, Gwen, Gwen, Gwen, I ask you finally—and all my life hangs upon the question—can you love me, will you love me, do you love me?'

Gwen let him fold her passionately in his arms as she murmured twice, almost inaudibly, 'I love you! I love you!'

Yes, yes, she couldn't any longer herself withstand the conviction. She loved him. She loved him.

As for Hiram, the blood thrilled through his veins as though his heart would burst for very fulness. The dream of his existence had come true at last, and he cared for nothing else on earth now he had once heard Gwen say with her own dear lips that she loved him, she loved him.

CHAPTER XL. AFTER THE STORM.

W hen Gwen told the colonel the very same evening that she had actually gone and got herself engaged to that shock-headed Yankee painter fellow, the colonel's wrath and grief and indignation were really something wonderful to observe and excellent to philosophise upon. The colonel raved, and stamped, and fretted; the colonel fumed in impotent rage, and talked grimly about his intentions and his paternal authority (just as if he had any); the colonel even swore strange Hindustani oaths at Gwen's devoted head, and supplemented them by all the choicest and most dignified military expletives to be found in the vocabulary of his native language. But Gwen remained perfectly unmoved by all the colonel's threats and imprecations; she flatly remarked that his testamentary dispositions were a subject in no way interesting or amusing to her, and stuck firm to her central contention, that it was she who was going to marry Hiram, and not her father, and that therefore she was the only person whose tastes and inclinations in the matter ought to be taken into any serious consideration. And though the colonel persisted in declaring that he for his part would never allow that Gwen was in any proper sense engaged to Hiram, Gwen herself stood to it stoutly that she *was* so engaged; and after all, her opinion on the subject was really by far the most important and conclusive of any.

In fact, the more the colonel declaimed against Hiram, the more profoundly convinced did Gwen become in her own heart that she thoroughly loved and admired him. And the final consequence of the colonel's violent opposition was merely this, that at the end of three weeks or so Gwen was as madly in love with her American painter fellow as any woman on this earth had ever yet been with a favoured lover.

As for poor Hiram, he was absolutely in the seventh heaven for the time being, and though a little later on he began to reproach himself bitterly at times for having tied down Gwen so prematurely to his own exceedingly doubtful fortunes, he could think as yet of nothing on earth but his delight at having actually won the love of the lady of his one long impassioned daydream.

On the day after Gwen had accepted Hiram's timid offer, Colin Churchill met Miss Howard-Russell accidentally in the Corso.

'Oh, Miss Russell,' he said, 'will you come on Sunday next to see my model, Cecca, married to her old Calabrian lover? She's very anxious you should come and assist, and she begged me most particularly to invite you. She says you're a friend of hers, and that the other day you did her and her lover a good service.'

'Tell her I'll be there, Mr. Churchill,' Gwen answered, smiling curiously, 'and tell her too that I have acted upon her advice, and she will understand you. Where's the wedding to be, and when must I be there?'

'At ten o'clock, close by our house, at Santa Maria of the Beautiful Ladies. She was to have been married a fortnight ago quite suddenly; but she changed her mind in a hurry at the last moment, because she hadn't got all her things ready. It'll be a dreadful loss to me, of course; for when once a model marries, you can never get her to sit again half as well as she used to do; but Cecca had a lover, it seems, who had followed her devotedly to Rome all the way from Monteleone; and she played fast-and-loose with him at first and rode the high horse, on the strength of her being so much admired and earning so much money as a model; and now she's seized with a sudden remorse, it appears, and wants to make it all up with him again and get married immediately.'

Gwen smiled a silent smile of quiet comprehension. 'I see,' she said. 'One can easily understand it. I shall be there, Mr. Churchill; you may depend upon me. And your cousin the —Miss Wroe, I mean—will she be there also?'

'Oh yes,' Colin answered lightly, 'Minna's coming too. She and Cecca have most mysteriously struck up quite a singular and sudden friendship.'

'I shall be glad to meet her again,' Gwen said simply. Somehow, when once one has settled firmly one's own affections, one feels a newborn and most benevolent desire to expedite to the best of one's abilities everybody else's little pending matrimonial arrangements.

So on Sunday Cecca was duly married, and the colonel and the earl were induced by Gwen to be present at the ceremony; though the colonel had his scruples upon the point, for, like most old Anglo-Indians of his generation, he was profoundly evangelical in his religious views, and regarded a Roman Catholic church as a place only to be visited under protest, by way of a show, with every decent expression of distaste and irreverence. Still, he knew his duty as a father; and when Gwen declared that if he didn't accompany her she would take Cousin Dick alone, and go without him, the colonel reflected wisely that she would probably meet that shock-headed Yankee painter fellow after the ceremony, and have another chance of talking over this absurd engagement she imagined she'd contracted with him. So he went himself to mount guard over her, and to give that Yankee fellow a piece of his mind if occasion offered.

And when the wedding was over, the whole party of guests, including Hiram and Audouin, adjourned for breakfast to the big room at Colin Churchill's studio, which had been laid out and decorated by Cecca and Minna and the people at the trattoria the evening before for that very purpose. And the Italian peasant folk sat by themselves at one end of the long wooden table, and the English excellencies also by themselves at the other. And Colin proposed the bride's health in his very best Tuscan: and Giuseppe made answer with native Italian eloquence in the nearest approach he could attain to the same exalted northerly dialect. And everybody said it was a great success, and even Cecca herself felt immensely proud and very happy. But I'm afraid my insular English readers will still harbour an unworthy prejudice against poor simple easy-going Calabrian Cecca, for no better reason than just because she tried, in a moment of ordinary Italian jealousy, to poison Minna Wroe in a cup of coffee. Such are the effects of truculent Anglo-Saxon narrowness and exclusiveness.

When Gwen and Minna went into Cecca's dressing-room to take off their bonnets (for Colin insisted that they should make a day of it), Gwen was suddenly moved by that benevolent instinct aforesaid to make a confidante of the pretty little governess—who, by the way, had got a new and more fashionable bonnet from a Roman Parisian milliner expressly for the happy occasion. Poor little thing! after all, it was very natural she should be dreadfully in love with her handsome clever sculptor cousin. 'I myself very nearly fell in love with him once, indeed,' Gwen murmured to herself philosophically, with the calm inner confidence of a newly-found affection. So she said to Minna with a meaning look, after a few arch little remarks about Colin's success as a rising sculptor, 'I have something to tell you, Miss Wroe, that I think will please you. I tell it to you because I know the subject is one you're much interested in; but, if you please you must treat it as a secret—a very great secret. I'm —well, to tell you the truth, Miss Wroe, I'm engaged to be married.'

Minna's face turned pale as death, and she gasped faintly,

but she answered nothing.

Gwen saw the cause of her anxiety at once, and hastened eagerly to reassure her.

'And if you'll promise not to say a word about it to anybody on earth, I'll tell you who it is—it's your cousin's American friend, Mr. Hiram Winthrop.'

Minna looked at her for a second in a transport of joy, and then burst suddenly into a flood of tears.

Gwen didn't for a moment pretend to misunderstand her. She knew what the tears meant, and she sympathised with them too deeply not to show her understanding frankly and openly. After all, the little governess was really at heart just a woman even as she herself was. 'There, there, dear,' she said, laying Minna's head upon her shoulder tenderly; 'cry on, cry on; cry as much as ever you want to; it'll do you good and relieve you. I know all about it, and I was sure you mistook me for a moment, and had got a wrong notion into your head, somehow; and that was why I took the liberty of telling you my little secret. It's all right, dear; don't be in the least afraid about it. Here, Cecca, quick; a glass of water!'

Cecca brought the water hastily, and then looking up with a wondering look into the tall Englishwoman's clear-cut face, she asked sternly, 'What is this you have been saying to the dear little signorina?'

'Gwen laid Minna down in a chair.'

Original

Gwen laid Minna down in a chair, after loosening her bonnet, and bathing her forehead with water; and then taking Cecca aside, she whispered to her softly, 'It's all right. Don't be afraid that I had forgotten or repented. I was telling her something that has pleased and delighted her. I am—I am going to be married, too, Cecca; but not to the master, to somebody else—to another artist, who has loved me for years, Signora Cecca; only mind, it's a secret, and you mustn't say a word for worlds to anybody about it.

Cecca smiled, and nodded knowingly. 'I see,' she said with a perfect shower of gestures. 'I see. It is well, indeed. To the American! Felicitations, signorina.'

'Hush, hush!' Gwen cried, putting her hand upon the beautiful model's mouth hastily. 'Not a word about it, I beg of you! Well now, dear, how are you feeling after the water? Are you better? are you better?'

'Thank you, Miss Russell; it was only a minute's faintness. I thought— — It's all right now. I'm better, Miss Russell, I'm better.'

Gwen looked at her tenderly as if she had been a sister. 'Your name's Minna, dear, I think,' she said; 'isn't it?'

Minna nodded acquiescence.

'And mine, I dare say you know, is Gwen. In future let us always call one another Gwen and Minna.'

She held out her arms caressingly, and Minna, forgetful at once of all her old wrath and jealousy of the grand young lady, nestled into them with a childlike look of unspeakable gratitude. 'It's very kind of you,' she cried, kissing Gwen's lull red lips two or three times over, 'so very, very kind of you. You can't tell how much you've relieved me, Miss Russell. You know— - I'm so very fond— — so very fond— — so very fond of dear Colin.'

Gwen kissed her in return sympathetically.

'I know you are, dear,' she answered warmly.

'And you needn't be afraid; I'm sure he loves you, he can't help loving you. You dear little thing, he must be a stone indeed if he doesn't love you. Cecca says he does, and Cecca's really a wonderful woman at finding out all these things immediately by a kind of instinct. But if ever you dare to call me Miss Russell again from this very minute forward, why, really, Minna, I solemnly declare I shall be awfully angry with you.'

Minna smiled and promised cheerfully. In truth, at that moment her heart was full to overflowing. Her rivals—both of her real or imaginary rivals—were at last safely disposed of, and if only now she could be perfectly sure that Colin loved her! Gwen said so, and Cecca said so, but Colin didn't. If only Colin would once say to her in so many words, 'Minna, I love you. Will you marry me?' Oh, how happy she would be, if only he would say so!

CHAPTER XLI. AUDOUIN'S MISTAKE.

L othrop Audouin walked round a little tremblingly to the Villa Panormi. He wasn't generally a shy or nervous man, but on this particular afternoon he felt an unwonted agitation in his breast, for he was bound to the Villa on a very special errand; and he was glad when he saw Gwen Howard-Russell walking about alone in the alleys of the garden, for it saved him the necessity of having to make a formal call upon her in the big salon. Gwen saw him coming, and moved towards the heavy iron gate to meet him.

She gave him her hand with one of her sunniest smiles, and Audouin took it, as he always did, with antique Massachusetts ceremoniousness. Then he turned with her, almost by accident as it were, down the path bordered by the orange-trees, and began to talk as he loved so well to talk, about the trees, and the flowers, and the green-grey lizards, that sat sunning themselves lazily upon the red Roman tiles which formed the stiff and formal garden edging.

'Though these are not my own flowers, you know, Miss Russell,' he said at last, looking at her a little curiously. 'These are not my own flowers; and indeed everything here in Rome, even nature itself, always seems to me so overlaid by the all-pervading influence of art that I fail to feel at home with the very lilies and violets in this artificial atmosphere In America, you know, my surroundings are so absolutely those of unmixed nature: I lead the life of a perfect hermit in an unsophisticated and undesecrated wilderness.'

'Mr. Winthrop has told me a great deal about Lakeside,' Gwen answered lightly, and Audouin took it as a good omen that she should have remembered the very name of his woodland cottage. 'You live quite among the primæval forest, don't you, by a big shallow bend in Lake Ontario?'

'Yes, quite among the primæval forest indeed; from my study window I look out upon nothing but the green pines, and the rocky ravine, and the great blue sheet of Ontario for an infinite background. Not a house or a sign of life to be seen anywhere, except the flying-squirrels darting about among the branches of the hickories.'

'But don't you get very tired and lonely there, with nobody but yourself and your servants? Don't you feel dreadfully the want of congenial cultivated society?'

Audouin sighed pensively to hide the beating of his heart at that simple question.

Surely, surely, the beautiful queenly Englishwoman was leading up to his hand! Surely she must know what was the natural interpretation for him to put upon her last inquiry! It is gross presumptuousness on the part of any man to ask a woman for the priceless gift of her whole future unless you have good reason to think that you are not wholly without hope of a favourable answer; but Gwen Howard-Russell must certainly mean to encourage him in the bold plunge he was on the verge of taking. It is hard for a chivalrous man to ask a woman that supreme question at any time: harder still when, like Lothrop Audouin, he has left it till time has begun to sprinkle his locks with silver. But Gwen was evidently not wholly averse to his proposition: he would break the ice between them and venture at last upon a declaration.

'Well,' he answered slowly, looking at Gwen half askance in a timid fashion very unlike his usual easy airy gallantry, 'I usen't to think it so, Miss Howard; I usen't to think it so. I had my books and my good companions—Plato, and Montaigne, and Burton, and Rabelais. I loved the woods and the flowers and the living creatures, and all my life long, you know, I have been a fool to nature, a fool to nature. Perhaps there was a little spice of misanthropy, too, in my desire to fly from a base, degrading, materialised civilisation. I didn't feel lonely in those days;—no, in those days, in those days, Miss Russell, I didn't feel lonely.'

He spoke hesitatingly, with long pauses between each little sentence, and his lips quivered as he spoke with girlish tremulousness and suppressed emotion. He who was usually so fluent and so ready with his rounded periods— he hardly managed now to frame his tongue to the few short words he wished to say to her. Profoundly and tenderly respectful by nature to all women, he felt so deeply awed by Gwen's presence and by the magnitude of the favour he wished to ask of her, that he trembled like a child as he tried to speak out boldly his heart's desire. It was not nervousness, it was not timidity, it was not diffidence; it was the overpowering emotion of a mature man, pent up till now, and breaking over him at last in a perfect inundation through the late-opened floodgates of his repressed passion. For a moment he leaned his hand against the projecting rockery of the grotto for support; then he spoke once more in a hushed voice, so that even Gwen vaguely suspected the real nature of his coming declaration.

'In those days,' he repeated once more, with knees failing under him for trembling, 'in those days I didn't feel lonely; but since my last visit to Rome I have felt Lakeside much more solitary than before. I have tired of my old crony Nature, and have begun to feel a newborn desire for closer human companionship. I have begun to wish for the presence of some kind and beautiful friend to share its pleasures with me. I needn't tell you, Miss Russell, why I date the uprising of that feeling from the time of my last visit to Italy. It was then that I first learned really to know and to admire you. It is a great thing to ask, I know, a

112

woman's heart—a true noble woman's whole heart and affection; but I dare to beg for it—I dare to beg for it. Oh, Miss Russell—oh, Gwen, Gwen, will you have pity upon me? will you give it me? will you give it me?' As he spoke, the tall strong-knit man, clutching the rock-work passionately for support, he looked so pale and faint and agitated that Gwen thought he would have fallen there and then, if she gave him the only possible answer too rudely and suddenly.

So she took his arm gently in hers, as a daughter might take a father's, and led him to the seat at the far end of the orange alley by the artificial fountain. Audouin followed her with a beating heart, and threw himself down half fainting on the slab of marble.

'Mr. Audouin,' Gwen began gently, for she pitied his evident overpowering emotion from the bottom of her heart, 'I can't tell you how sorry I am to have to say so, but it cannot possibly be; it can never be, never, so it's no use my trying to talk about it.'

A knife struck through Audouin's bosom at those simple words, and he grew still paler white than ever, but he merely bowed his head respectfully, and, crushing down his love with iron resolution, murmured slowly, 'Then forgive me, forgive me.' His unwritten creed would not have permitted him in such circumstances to press his broken suit one moment longer.

'Mr. Audouin,' Gwen went on, 'I'm afraid I have unintentionally misled you. No, I don't want you to go yet,' she added with one of her imperious gestures, for he seemed as if he would rise and leave her; 'I don't want you to go until I have explained it all to you. I like you very much, I have always liked you; I respect you, too, and I've been pleased and proud of the privilege of your acquaintance. Perhaps in doing so much, in seeking to talk with you and

113

enjoy your society, I may have seemed to have encouraged you in feelings which it never struck me you were at all likely to harbour. I—I liked you so sincerely that I never even dreamt you might fancy I could love you.' 'And why, Miss Russell?' Audouin pleaded earnestly. 'If you dismiss me so hopelessly, let me know at least the reason of my dismissal. It was very presumptuous of me, I know, to dare to hope for so much happiness; but why did you think me quite outside the sphere of your possible suitors?'

'Why, Mr. Audouin,' Gwen said in a low tone, 'I have always looked upon you rather as one might look upon a father than as one might look upon a young man of one's own generation. I never even thought of you before to-day except as somebody so much older and wiser, and altogether different from myself, that it didn't occur to me for a single moment you yourself wouldn't feel so also.' Audouin's despairing face brightened a little as he said, 'If that is all, Miss Russell, mayn't I venture to look upon your answer as not quite final; mayn't I hope to leave the question open yet a little, so that you may see what time may do for me, now you know my inmost feeling? Don't crush me hopelessly at once; let me linger a little before you utterly reject me. If you only knew how deeply you have entwined yourself into my very being, you wouldn't cast me off so lightly and so easily.'

Gwen looked at him with a face full of unfeigned pity. 'Mr. Audouin,' she answered, 'I know how truly you are speaking. I should read your nature badly if I didn't see it in your very eyes. But I cannot hold you out any hope in any way. I like you immensely; I feel profoundly sorry to have to speak so plainly to you. I know how great an honour you confer upon me by your offer; but I can't accept it—it's quite impossible that I can ever accept it. I like you, and respect you more than I ever liked or respected any other person, except one; but there is one person I like and respect even

114

more, so you see at once why it's quite impossible that I should listen to you about this any longer.'

'I understand,' Audouin answered slowly. 'I understand. I see it all now. Colin Churchill has been beforehand with me. While I hesitated, he has acted.'

Gwen's lips broke for a moment into a quiet smile, and she murmured softly, 'No, not Colin Churchill, Mr. Audouin, not Colin Churchill, but Hiram Winthrop. I think, as I have said so much, I ought to tell you it is Hiram Winthrop.'

Audouin's brain reeled round madly in grief and indignation at that astonishing revelation. Hiram Winthrop! His own familiar friend; his dearest ward and pupil! Was it he, then, who had stolen this prize of life, unseen, unsuspected, beneath his very eyesight? If Gwen had never fancied that Audouin could fall in love with her, neither could Audouin ever have suspected it of Hiram Winthrop. If Gwen had looked upon Audouin as a confirmed old bachelor of the elder generation, Audouin had looked upon Hiram as a mere boy, too young yet to meddle with such serious fancies. And now the boy had stolen Gwen from him unawares, and for half a second, all loyal as he was, Audouin felt sick and angry in soul at what he figured to himself as Hiram's cruel and ungrateful duplicity.

'Hiram Winthrop!' he muttered angrily. 'Hiram Winthrop! How unworthy of him! how unkind of him! how unjust of him to come between me and the one object he ever knew me set my heart upon!'

'But, Mr. Audouin,' Gwen cried in warmer tones, 'Hiram no more dreamt of this than I did; he took it for granted all along that you knew he loved me, but he never spoke of it because you know he is always reserved about everything that concerns his own personal feelings.'

The marble seat reeled and the ground shook beneath Audouin's feet as he sat there, his brow between his hands, and his elbows upon his knees, trying to realise the true bearings of what Gwen was saying to him. Yes, he saw it all plainly now; it dawned upon him slowly: in his foolish, selfish, blind preoccupation, he had been thinking only of his own love, and wholly overlooking Gwen's and Hiram's. 'What a short-sighted fool I have been, Miss Russell!' he cried, broken-spirited. 'Yes, yes; Hiram is not to blame. I only am to blame for my own folly. If Hiram loves you, and you love Hiram, I have only one duty left before me: to leave you this moment, and to do whatever in me lies to make you and Hiram as happy as I can. No two people on this earth have ever been dearer to me. I must try to change my attitude to you both, and learn that I am old enough to help even now to make you happy.' In his perfect loyalty, Audouin almost forgot at once his passing twinge of distrust for Hiram, and thought only of his own blindness. He rose slowly from the marble seat, and Gwen noticed that as he rose he seemed to have aged visibly in those few minutes. The suddenness and utterness of the disappointment had unmistakably crushed him. He staggered a little as he rose; then in a faltering voice he said, 'Good-bye, good-bye, Miss Russel.' Gwen turned away her face, and answered regretfully, 'Good-bye, Mr. Audouin.'

He raised his hat, with a touch of old-fashioned courtesy in his formal bow, and walked away quickly, out of the garden, and back towards the hotel where he had been then stopping. For some time his disappointment sat upon him so heavily that he could only brood over it in a vague, half unconscious fashion; but at last, as he passed the corner of the big piazza a thought seemed to flash suddenly across his dazzled brain, and he turned round at once, in feverish haste, pacing back moodily towards the Villa Panormi. 'How selfish of me!' he said to himself in angry self-expostulation, 'how selfish and cruel of me to have forgotten it! How small and narrow and petty we men are, after all! In my dejection at my own disappointment, I have quite overlooked poor Hiram. Love may be all that the poets say about it—I don't know, I can't say—how should I, a lonely wild man of the woods, who know not the ways of women? But one thing I do know: it's a terrible absorbing and self-centring passion. A man thinks only of him and her, and forgets all the rest of the world entirely, as though he were a solitary savage wooing in the gloom his solitary squaw. And yet they write about it as though it were the very head and front of all the beatitudes!'

He walked, or almost ran, to the Villa Panormi, and looked anxiously for Gwen in the alleys of the garden. She wasn't there: she had gone in evidently. He must go to the door and boldly ask for her. Was the signorina at home, he enquired of the servant. Yes, the signorina had just come in: what name, signor? Audouin handed the man his card, and waited with a burning heart in the long open salon.

In a minute Gwen sent down word by her English maid: she was very sorry; would Mr. Audouin kindly excuse her? —she was suffering from headache.

'Tell Miss Russell,' Audouin answered, so earnestly that the girl guessed at once something of his business, 'that I *must* see her without delay. The matter is important, immediate, urgent, and of more interest to her than even to me.'

He waited again for fully ten minutes. Then Gwen sailed into the room, queen-like as ever, and advanced towards him smiling; but he saw she had been crying, and had bathed her eyes to hide it, and he felt flattered in his heart even then at that womanly tribute of sympathy to his bitter disappointment. 'Miss Russell,' he said, with all the sincerity of his inner nature speaking vividly in his very voice, 'I am

117

more sorry than I can say that I'm compelled to come back so soon and speak with you again after what has just happened. We may still be always firm friends, I'm sure; I shall try to feel towards you always as an elder brother: but I know you would have liked a day or two to pass before we met again on what is to me at least a new footing. Still, I felt compelled to come back and tell you something which it is of great importance that you should know at once. Miss Bussell, you mustn't on any account breathe a word of all this in any way to Hiram. Don't think I'm speaking without good reason. As you value your own happiness, don't breathe a word of it to Hiram.'

Gwen saw from his exceeding earnestness that he had some definite ground for this odd warning, and it piqued her curiosity to know what that ground could possibly be. 'Why, Mr. Audouin?' she asked simply.

'Because it would cause you great distress, I believe,' Audouin answered evasively. 'Because it would probably prevent his ever marrying you. Oh, Miss Russell, do please promise me that you'll say nothing at all to him about it.'

'But I can't promise, Mr. Audouin,' Gwen answered slowly. 'I can't promise. I feel I ought to tell him. I think a woman ought to tell her future husband everything.'

'Miss Russell,' Audouin went on, still more solemnly than before, 'I beg of you, I implore you, I beseech you, for the sake of your own future and Hiram's, don't say a word to him of this.'

'But why, why, Mr. Audouin? You give me no reason, no explanation. If you won't explain to me, you'll only frighten me the more into telling Hiram, because your manner seems so excited and so mysterious. I can't promise or refuse to promise until I understand what you mean by it.'

'I had rather not explain to you,' Audouin went on hesitatingly. 'I should prefer not to have told you. Indeed, unless you compel me, I will never tell you. But from my own knowledge of Hiram's character I feel sure that if you let him know about this he will never, never marry you. He is so unselfish, so good, so delicately self-sacrificing, that if he hears of this he will think he mustn't claim you. I have known him, Miss Russell, longer than you have; I can count better on what he would do under any given circumstances. Most men are selfish and blind in love; I was so just now: I have been all along, when in my personal eagerness to win your esteem I never noticed what was indeed as clear as daylight, that Hiram must have been in love with you too. But Hiram is not selfish and blind, even in love; of that I'm certain. He would never marry you if he thought that by so doing he was putting himself in rivalry with me.'

'And why not?' Gwen asked, with her large eyes looking through and through Audouin's to their very centre. 'Why not with you in particular?'

'Because,' Audouin answered, faltering, and trying to withdraw his gaze from hers, but unsuccessfully, for she seemed to mesmerise him with her keen glance, 'because, Miss Bussell, if you force me to tell you, I have been of some little service at various times to Hiram, and have placed him under some slight obligations, whose importance his generous nature vastly overestimates. I am quite sure, from what I know of him, that if he thought I had ever dreamt of the possibility of asking you to put up with my poor little individuality, he would never feel himself at liberty to marry you; he would think he was being unfriendly and (as he would say) ungrateful. I dare say you will fancy to yourself that I am making him out but a cold lover. I am not, Miss Russell; I am giving him the highest praise in my power. I feel confident that, though he loved you as the apple of his eye, he wouldn't sacrifice what he thought honour and duty even for your sake.'

Gwen looked at him steadily, and answered in a trembling voice, 'I will say nothing to him about it, Mr. Audouin, nothing at all until after we are married. Then, you know, then I *must* tell him.'

'Thank you,' Audouin said gently. 'That will do sufficiently. Thank you, thank you. If it hadn't been a matter of such urgency I wouldn't have troubled you with it now. But as I went along the road homeward, heavy at heart, as you may imagine, it struck me like a flash of lightning that you might speak to Hiram about it this very day, and that Hiram, if he heard it, might withdraw his pretensions, so to speak, and feel compelled to retire in my favour. And as he loves you, and as you love him, I should never have forgiven myself if that had happened—had even momentarily happened. You will have difficulties and perplexities enough in any case without my adding my mite to them, I feel certain. And I was so appalled at my own wicked selfishness in having overlooked all this, that I felt constrained to come back, even at the risk of offending you, and set the matter at rest this very afternoon. I won't detain you a moment longer now. Good-bye, Miss Russell, good-bye, and thank you.'

Gwen looked at him again as he stood there, with his face so evidently pained with the lasting pain of his great disappointment, utterly oblivious of self even at that supreme hour in his thought for his friend, yet reproaching himself so unfeignedly for his supposed selfishness, and she thought as she looked how truly noble he was at heart after all. The outer shell of affectation and mannerism was all gone now, and the true inner core of the man lay open before her in all its beautiful trustful simplicity. At that moment Gwen Howard-Russell felt as if she really loved Lothrop Audouin—loved him as a daughter might love a pure, generous, tender father. She looked at him steadily for a minute as he stood there with his hand outstretched for hers, and then, giving way to her natural womanly impulse for one second, she cried, 'Oh, Mr. Audouin, I mustn't love you, I mustn't love you; but I can't tell you how deeply I respect and admire you!' And as she spoke, to Audouin's intense surprise and joy—yes, joy—she laid both her hands tenderly upon his shoulders, drew him down to her unresisting, and kissed him once upon the face as she had long ago kissed her lost and all but forgotten mother. Then, with crimson cheeks, and eyes flooded with tears, she rushed away, astonished and half angry with herself for the audacious impulse, yet proudly beautiful as ever, leaving Audouin alone and trembling in the empty salon.

Audouin was too pure at heart himself not to accept the kiss exactly as it was intended. He drew himself up once more, ashamed of the fluttering in his unworthy bosom, which he could not help but feel; and saying in his own soul gently, 'Poor little guileless heart! she takes me for better than I am, and treats me accordingly,' he sallied forth once more into the narrow gloomy streets of Rome, and walked away hurriedly, he cared not whither.

CHAPTER XLII. A DISTINGUISHED CRITIC.

It was a very warm morning in the Via Colonna, for many weeks had passed, and May was coming on: it was a warm morning, and Hiram was plodding away drearily by himself at his heroic picture of the Capture of Babylon, with a stalwart young Roman from the Campagna sitting for his model of the Persian leader, when the door unexpectedly opened, and a quiet-looking old gentleman entered suddenly, alone and unannounced. This was one of Hiram's days of deepest despondency, and he was heartily sorry for the untimely interruption. 'Mr. Churchill sent me to look at your pictures.' the stranger said in explanation, in a very soft, pleasant voice. 'He told me I might possibly see some things here that were really worth the looking at.'

Poor Hiram sighed somewhat wearily. 'Churchill has too good an opinion altogether of my little attempts,' he said in all sincerity.

'I'm afraid you'll find very little here that's worthy your attention. May I venture to ask your name?'

'Never mind my name, sir,' the old gentleman said, with a blandness that contrasted oddly with the rough wording of his brusque sentences. 'Never you mind my name, I say,— what's that to you, pray? My name's not at all in question. I've come to see your pictures.'

'Are you a dealer, perhaps?' Hiram suggested, with another sigh at his own excessive frankness in depreciating what was after all his bread and butter—and a great deal more to him. 'You want to buy possibly?

'No, I don't want to buy,' the old gentleman answered

flatly, with a certain mild and kindly fierceness. 'I don't want to buy certainly. I'm not a dealer; I'm an art-critic.'

'Oh, indeed,' Hiram said politely. The qualification is not one usually calculated to endear a visitor to a struggling young artist.

'And you, I should say by your accent, are an American. That's bad, to begin with. What on earth induced you to leave that cursed country of yours? Oh generation of vipers —don't misinterpret that much-mistaken word generation; it means merely son or offspring—who has warned you to flee from the wrath that is?'

Hiram smiled in spite of himself. 'Myself,' he said; 'my own inner prompting only.'

'Ha, that's better; so you fled from it.

You escaped from the city of destruction. You saved yourself from Sodom and Gomorrah. Well, well, having had the misfortune to be born an American, what better thing could you possibly do? Creditable, certainly, very creditable. And now, since you have come to Rome to paint, pray what sort of wares have you got to show me?'

Hiram pointed gravely to the unfinished Capture of Babylon.

'It won't do,' the old gentleman said decisively, after surveying the principal figures with a critical eye through his double eyeglass. 'Oh, no, it won't do at all. It's painted— I admit that; it's painted, solidly painted, which is always something nowadays, when coxcombs go splashing their brushes loosely about a yard or two of blank canvas, and then positively calling it a picture. It's painted, there's no denying it. Still, my dear sir, you'll excuse my saying so, but there's really nothing in it—absolutely nothing. What does it amount to, after all? A line farrago of tweedledum and tweedledee, in Assyrian armour and Oriental costume, and other unnatural, incongruous upholsterings, with a few

Roman models stuck inside it all, to do duty instead of lay figures. Do you really mean to tell me, now, you think *that* was what the capture of Babylon actually looked like? Why, my dear sir, speaking quite candidly, I assure you, for my own part I much prefer the Assyrian bas-reliefs.'

Hiram's heart sank horribly within him. He knew it, he knew it; it was all an error, a gigantic error. He had mistaken a taste for painting for a genius for painting. He would never, never, never make a painter; of that he was now absolutely certain. He could have sat down that moment with his face between his hands and cried bitterly, even as he had done years before when the deacon left him in the peppermint lot, but for the constraining presence of that mild-mannered ferocious oddly-compounded old gentleman.

'Is this any better?' he asked humbly, pointing with his brush-handle to the Second Triumvirate.

'No sir, it is *not* any better,' the relentless critic answered as fiercely yet as blandly as ever. 'In fact, if it comes to that, it's a great deal worse. Look at it fairly in the face and ask yourself what it all comes to. It's a group of three amiable sugar-brokers in masquerade costume discussing the current price-lists, and it isn't even painted, though it's by way of being finished, I suppose, as people paint nowadays. Is *that* drawing, for example,' and he stuck his forefinger upon young Cæsar's foreshortened foot, 'or that, or that, or that, or that, sir? Oh, no, no; dear me, no. This is nothing like either drawing or colouring. The figure, my dear sir— you'll excuse my saying so, but you haven't the most rudimentary conception even of drawing or painting the human figure.'

Hiram coincided so heartily at that moment in this vigorous expression of adverse opinion, that but for Gwen he could have pulled out his pocket-knife on the spot and made a brief end of a life long failure.

But the stranger only went coolly through the studio piece by piece, passing the same discouraging criticisms upon everything he saw, and after he had finally reduced poor Hiram to the last abyss of unutterable despair, he said pleasantly in his soft, almost womanly voice, 'Well, well, these are all sad trash, sad trash certainly. Not worth coming from America to Rome to paint, you must admit; certainly not. Who on earth was blockhead enough to tell you that you could ever possibly paint the figure? I don't understand this. Churchill's an artist; Churchill's a sculptor; Churchill knows what a human body's like, he's no fool, I know. What the deuce did he send me here for, I wonder? How on earth could he ever have imagined that those stuffed Guy Fawkeses and wooden marionettes and dancing fantoccini were real living men and women? Preposterous, preposterous. Stay. Let me think. Churchill said something or other about your trying landscape. Have you got any landscapes, young man, got any landscapes?'

'I've a few back here,' Hiram answered timidly, 'but I'm afraid they're hardly worth your serious consideration. They were mostly done before I left America, with very little teaching, or else on holidays here in Europe, in the Tyrol chiefly, without much advice or assistance from competent masters.'

'Bring them out!' the old gentleman said in a tone of command. 'Produce your landscapes. Let's see what this place America is like, this desert of newfangled towns without, any castles.'

Hiram obeyed, and brought out the poor little landscapes, sticking them one after another on the easel in the light. There were the Thousand Island sketches, and the New York lakes, and the White Mountains, and a few pine-clad glens and dingles among the Tyrolese uplands and the

125

lower Engadine. The stranger surveyed them all attentively through his double eyeglass with a stony critical stare, but still said absolutely nothing. Hiram stood by in breathless expectation. Perhaps the landscapes might fare better at this mysterious person's unsparing hands than the figure pieces. But no: when he had finished, the stranger only said calmly, 'Is that all?'

'All, all,' Hiram murmured in blank despair. 'The work of my lifetime.'

The stranger looked at him steadily.

'Young man,' he said with the voice and manner of a Hebrew prophet, 'believe me, you ought never to have come away from your native America.'

'I know it, I know it,' Hiram cried, in the profoundest depth of self-abasement.

'No, you ought never to have come away from America. As I wrote years ago in the Seven Domes of Florence——'

'What!' Hiram exclaimed, horror-stricken.

'The Seven Domes of Florence! Then—then—then you are Mr. Truman?'

'Yes,' the stranger went on unmoved, without heeding his startled condition. 'My name is John Truman, and, as I wrote years ago in the Seven Domes of Florence——'

Hiram never heard the end of his visitor's long sonorous quotation from his former self (in five volumes), for he sank back unmanned into an easy-chair, and fairly moaned aloud in the exceeding bitterness of his disappointment.

John Truman! It was he, then, the great art-critic of the age; the man whose merest word, whose slightest breath could make or mar a struggling reputation; the detector of fashionable shams, the promoter of honest artistic workmanship—it was he that had pronounced poor Hiram's whole life a miserable failure, and had remitted him

126

remorselessly once more to the corn and potatoes of Geauga County. The tears filled Hiram's eyes as he showed the great man slowly and regretfully out of his studio; and when that benevolent beaming face had disappeared incongruously with the parting Parthian shot, 'Go back to your woods and forests, sir; go back immediately to your woods and forests,' Hiram quite forgot the very presence of the decked-out Persian commander, and burst into hot tears such as he had not shed before since he ran away to nurse his boyish sorrows alone by himself in the old familiar blackberry bottom.

How very differently he might have felt if only he could have followed that stooping figure down the Via Colonna and heard the bland old gentleman muttering audibly to himself, 'Oh, dear no, the young barbarian ought never to have come away from his native America. No castles— certainly not, but there's nature there clearly, a great deal of nature; and he knows how to paint it too, he knows how to paint it. Great purity of colouring in his Tyrolese sketches; breadth and brilliancy very unusual in so young an artist; capital robust drawing; a certain glassy liquid touch that I like about it all, too, especially in the water. Who on earth ever told him to go and paint those incomprehensible Assyrian monstrosities? Ridiculous, quite ridiculous. He ought to have concentrated himself on his own congenial lakes and woodlands. He has caught the exact spirit of them—weird, mysterious, solemn, primitive, unvulgarised, antidemotic, titanic, infinite. The draughtsmanship of the stratification in the rocks is quite superb in its originality. Oh, dear no, he ought never to have come away at all from his native natural America.

CHAPTER XLIII. THE SLOUGH OF DESPOND.

Mr. Audouin,' Hiram cried, bursting into his friend's rooms in a fever of despair, three days later, 'I've come to tell you I'm going back to America!'

'Back to America, Hiram!' Audouin cried in dismay, for he guessed the cause instinctively at once. 'Why, what on earth do you want to do that for?'

Hiram flung himself back in moody dejection on the ottoman in the corner. 'Why,' he said, 'do you know who has been to see me? Mr. Truman.'

'Well, Hiram?' Audouin murmured, trembling.

'Well, he tells me I've made a complete mistake of it. I'm not a painter, I can't be a painter, and I never could possibly make a painter. Oh, Mr. Audouin, Mr. Audouin, I knew it myself long ago, but till this very week I've hoped against hope, and never ventured fully to realise it. But I know now he tells the truth. I can't paint, I tell you, I can't paint—no, not that much!' And he snapped his fingers bitterly in his utter humiliation.

Audouin drew a chair over softly to his friend's side, and laid his hand with womanly tenderness upon the listless arm. 'Hiram,' he said in a tone of deep self-reproach, 'it's all my fault; my fault, and mine only. I am to blame for all this. I wanted to help and direct and encourage you; and in the end, I've only succeeded in making both of us supremely miserable!'

'Oh, no,' Hiram cried, taking Audouin's hand warmly in his own, 'not your fault, dear Mr. Audouin, not your fault, nor mine, but nature's. You thought there was more in me than there actually was—that was kindly and friendly and well-meant of you. You fancied you had found an artistic genius, an oasis in the sandy desert of Geauga County, and you wanted to develop and assist him. It was generous and noble of you; if you were misled, it was your own sympathetic, appreciative, disinterested nature that misled you. You were too enthusiastic. You always thought better of me than I have ever thought of myself; but if that's a fault, it's a fault on the nobler side, surely. No, no, nobody is to blame for this but myself, my own feeble self, that cannot rise, whatever I may do, to the difficult heights you would have me fly to.' Audouin looked at him long and silently. In his own heart, he had begun to feel that Hiram's heroic figure-painting had turned out a distinct failure For that figure-painting he, Lotlirop Audouin, was alone responsible. But, even in spite of the great name of Truman urged against him, he could hardly believe that Hiram would not yet succeed in landscape. 'Did Truman see the Tyrolese sketches?' he asked anxiously at last.

'Yes, he did, Mr. Audouin.'

'And what did he say about them?'

'Simply that he thought I ought never to have come away from America.'

Audouin drew a long breath. 'This is very serious, Hiram,' he said slowly. 'I apprehend certainly that this is very serious. Truman's opinion is worth a great deal; but, after all, it isn't everything. I've led you wrong so long and so often, my poor boy, that I'm almost afraid to advise you any farther; and yet, do you know, I can't help somehow believing that you will really do great things yet in landscape.'

'Never, never,' Hiram answered firmly.

'I shall never do anything better than the edge of the lake at Chattawauga!'

'But you *have* done great things, Hiram,' Audouin cried, warming up with generous enthusiasm, just in proportion as his protégés spirits sank lower and lower. 'My dear fellow, you *have* done great things already. I'll stake my reputation upon it, Hiram, that the lake shore at Chattawauga's a piece of painting that'll even yet live and be famous.' Hiram shook his head gloomily. 'No, no,' he said; 'I mean to take Mr. Truman's advice, and go back to hoe corn and plant potatoes in Muddy Creek Valley. That's just about what I'm fit for.'

'But, Hiram,' his friend said, coming closer and closer to him, 'you mustn't dream of doing that. In justice to me you really mustn't. I've misled you and wasted your time, I know, by inducing you to go in for this wretched figure-painting. It doesn't suit you and your idiosyncrasy: that I see now quite clearly. All my life long it's been a favourite doctrine of mine, my boy, that the only true way of salvation lies in perfect fidelity to one's own inner promptings. And how have I carried out that gospel of mine in your case? Why, by absurdly inducing you to neglect the line you naturally excel in, and to take up with a line that you don't personally care a pin for. Now, dear Hiram, my dear, good fellow, don't go and punish me for this by returning in a huff to Geauga County. Have pity upon me, and spare me this misery, this degradation. I've suffered much already, though you never knew it, about this false direction I've tried to give your genius (for you *have* genius, I'm sure you have): I've lain awake night after night and reproached myself for it bitterly: don't go now and put me to shame by making my mistake destroy your whole future career and chances as a painter. It need cost you nothing to remain. I misled you by getting you to paint those historical subjects. I see they were a mistake now, and I will buy the whole of them from you at your own valuation. That will be only just, for it was for me really that you originally

painted them. Do, do please reconsider this hasty decision.'
Hiram rocked himself to and fro piteously upon the
ottoman, but only answered, 'Impossible, impossible. You
are too kind, too generous.'

Audouin looked once more at his dejected dispirited face,
and then, pausing a minute or two, said quietly and
solemnly, 'And how about Gwen, Hiram?'

Hiram started up in surprise and discomfiture, and asked
hastily, 'Why, what on earth do you know about Gwen—
about Miss Russell, I mean—Mr. Audouin?'

'I can't tell you how I've surprised your secret, Hiram,'
Audouin said, his voice trembling a little as he spoke:
'perhaps some day I may tell you, and perhaps never. But
I've found it all out, and I ask you, my boy, for Gwen's sake
—for Miss Russell's sake—to wait awhile before returning so
rashly to America. Hiram, you owe it as a duty to her not
to run away from her, and fame and fortune, at the first
failure.'

Hiram flung himself down upon the ottoman again in a
frenzy of despondency. 'That's just why I think I must go at
once, Mr. Audouin,' he cried, in his agony. 'I only know
two alternatives. One is America; the other is the Tiber.'

'Hiram, Hiram!' his friend said soothingly. 'Yes, yes, Mr.
Audouin, I know all that, I know what you want to say to
me. But I can't drag down Gwen—born and brought up as
she has been—I can't drag her down with me to a
struggling painter's pot-boiling squalidness. I can't do it,
and I won't do it, and I oughtn't to do it; and the kindest
thing for her sake, and for all our sakes, would be for me to
get out of it all at once and altogether.'

'Then you *will* go, Hiram?'

'Yes, I *will* go, Mr. Audouin, by the very next Trieste
steamer.'

He rose slowly from the ottoman, shook his friend's hand in silence, and went away without another word. Audouin saw by his manner that he really meant it, and he sat down wondering what good he could do to countervail this great unintentional evil he had done to Hiram.

'Lothrop Audouin,' he said to himself harshly, 'a pretty mess you have made now of your own life and of Hiram Winthrop's! Is this your perfect fidelity to the inner promptings—this your obedience to the unspoken voice of the divine human consciousness? You poor, purblind, affected, silly, weak, useless creature, I hate you, I hate you. Go, now, see what you can do to render happy these two better lives that you have done your best to ruin for ever.'

If any other man had used such words of Lothrop Audouin, he would have shown himself a bitter, foolish, short-sighted cynic. But as Lothrop Audouin said it himself, of course he had a full right to his own opinion.

Yet some men, not wholly bad men either, might have rejoiced at the thought that they would thus get rid of a successful rival. They would have said to themselves, 'When Hiram is gone, Gwen will soon forget him, and then I may have a chance at least of finally winning her favour.' In this belief, they would have urged Hiram, in a halfhearted way only, not to return to America; and if afterwards he persisted in his foolish intention, they might have said to themselves, 'I did my best to keep him, and now I wash my hands forever of it.' All's fair, says the proverb, in love and war; and many men still seem to think so. But Audouin was made of different mould; and having once frankly wooed and lost Gwen, he had no single shadow of a thought now left in his chivalrous mind save how to redress this great wrong he conceived he had done them, and how to make Gwen and Hiram finally happy.

He sat there long, musing and wondering, beating out a

plan of action for himself in his own brain, till at last he saw some gleam of hope clear before him. Then he rose, took down his hat quickly from the peg, and hurried round to Colin Churchill's studio. He found Colin working away busily at the moist clay of Agamemnon and Clytemnestra.

'Churchill,' he said seriously, 'you must put away your work for an hour. I want to speak to you about something very important.'

Colin laid down his graver reluctantly, and turned to look at his unexpected visitor.

'Why, great heavens, Mr. Audouin,' he said, 'what can be the matter with you? You really look as white as that marble.'

'Matter enough, Churchill. Who do you think has been to see Winthrop? Why, John Truman.'

'Oh, I know,' Colin answered cheerfully. 'I sent him myself. And what did he say then?'

'He said that Winthrop ought to go back to America, and that he would never, never, never make a decent painter.'

Colin whistled to himself quickly, and then said, 'The dickens he did! How remarkable! But did Winthrop show him the landscapes?' 'Yes, and from what he says, Truman seems to have thought worse of them than even he thought of the figure pieces.'

'Impossible!' Colin cried incredulously. 'I don't believe it; I can't believe it. Truman knows a landscape when he sees it. There must be some mistake somewhere.'

'I'm afraid not,' Audouin answered sadly. 'I've begun to despair about poor Winthrop myself, a great deal of late, and to reproach myself terribly for the share I've had in putting his genius on the wrong metals. The thing we've got to do now is to face the actuality, and manage the best we can for him under the circumstances. Churchill, do you know, Hiram threatens to go back to America by the next steamer, and take to farming for a livelihood.'

Colin whistled low again. 'He mustn't be allowed to do it,' he said quickly. 'He must be kept in Rome at all hazards. If we have to lock him up in jail or put him into a lunatic asylum, we must keep him here for the present, whatever comes of it. I'm sure as I am of anything, Mr. Audouin, that Hiram Winthrop has a splendid future still before him.'

'Well, Churchill,' Audouin said calmly, 'I want you to help me in a little scheme I've decided upon. I'm going to make my will, and I want you to be trustee under it.'

'Make your will, Mr. Audouin! Why, what on earth has that to do with Hiram Winthrop? I hope you'll live for many years yet, to see him paint whole square yards of splendid pictures.'

Audouin smiled a little sadly. 'It's well to be prepared against all contingencies,' he said with a forced gaiety of tone: 'and I want to provide against one which seems to me by no means improbable. There's no knowing when any man may die. Don't the preachers tell us that our life hangs always by a thread, and that the sword of Damocles is suspended forever above us?'

Colin looked at him keenly and searchingly. Audouin met his gaze with frank open eyes, and did not quail for a moment before his evident curiosity. 'Well, Churchill,' he went on more gravely, 'I'm going to make my will, and I'll tell you how I'm going to make it. I propose to leave all my property in trust to you, as a charity in perpetuity. I intend that you shall appoint some one young American artist as Audouin Art Scholar at Home, and pay to him the interest on that property, so long as he considers that he stands in need of it. As soon as he, by the exercise of his profession, is earning such an income that he feels he can safely do without it, then I leave it to him and you to choose some

135

other American Art student for the scholarship, to be enjoyed in like manner. On that second student voluntarily vacating the scholarship, you, he, and the first student shall similarly choose a third incumbent; and so on for ever. What do you think of the plan, Churchill, will it hold water?'

'But why shouldn't you leave it outright to Winthrop?' Colin asked, a little puzzled by this apparently roundabout proceeding. 'Wouldn't it be simpler and more satisfactory to give it to him direct, instead of in such a complicated fashion?'

'Who said a word about Winthrop being the first scholar?' Audouin answered with grave irony. 'You evidently misunderstand the spirit of the bequest. I want to advance American art, not to make a present to Hiram Winthrop. Besides,' and here Audouin lowered his voice a little more confidentially, 'if I left it to Hiram outright, I feel pretty confident he wouldn't accept it; he'd refuse the bequest as a personal matter. I know him, Churchill, better than you do; I know his proud sensitive nature, and the way he would shrink from accepting a fortune as a present even from a dead man—even from me, his most intimate friend and spiritual father. But if it's left in this way, he can hardly refuse; it will be only for a few years, till he gets his name up; it'll leave him free meanwhile to live and marry (if he wants to), and it'll be burdened with a condition, too— that he should go on studying and practising art, and that he should assist at the end of his own tenure in electing another scholar. That, I hope, would reconcile him (if the scholarship were offered to him) to the necessity of accepting and using it for a few years only. However, I don't wish, Churchill, to suggest any person whatsoever to you as the first student; I desire to leave your hands perfectly free and untied in that matter.'

'I see; I understand,' Cohn answered, smiling gently to himself. 'I will offer it, should the occasion ever arise, to the most promising young American student that I can anywhere discover.'

'Quite right, Churchill; exactly what I wish you to do. Then you'll accept the trust, and carry it out for me, will you?

'On one condition only, Mr. Audouin,' Colin said firmly, looking into his blanched face and straining eyeballs. 'On one condition only. Let me be quite frank with you—no suicide.'

Audouin started a little. 'Why, that's a fair enough proviso,' he answered slowly after a moment. 'Yes, I promise that. No suicide. We shall trust entirely to the chapter of accidents.'

'In that case,' Colin continued, reassured, 'I hope we may expect that the trusteeship will be a sinecure for many a long year to come. But I fail to see how all this will benefit poor Winthrop in the immediate future, if he means to sail for New York by the next steamer.'

'The two questions ought to be kept entirely distinct,' Audouin went on sharply, with perfect gravity. 'I fail myself to perceive how any possible connection can exist between them. Still, we will trust to the chapter of accidents. There's no knowing what a day may bring forth. We must try at least to keep Wintlirop here in Rome for another fortnight. That's not so very long to stay, and yet a great deal may be done in a fortnight. I'll go and look out at once for an American lawyer to draft my will for me. Meanwhile, will you just sign this joint note from both of us to Winthrop?'

He sat down hurriedly at Cohn's desk, and scribbled off a short note to poor Hiram.

'Dear Winthrop,—Will you as a personal favour to us both kindly delay your departure from Rome for another fortnight, by which time we hope we may be able to make different arrangements for you?

'Lothrop Audouin.'

He passed the note to Colin, and the pen with it. Colin read the doubtfully worded note over twice in a hesitating manner, and then, after some mental deliberation, added below in his clear masculine hand—'Colin Churchill.'

'Remember, Mr. Audouin,' he said as a parting warning. 'It's a bargain between us. No suicide.'

'Oh, all right,' Audouin answered lightly with the door in his hand. 'We trust entirely to the chapter of accidents.'

CHAPTER XLIV. THE CHAPTER OF ACCIDENTS.

Next day, after seeing the American lawyer (caught by good luck at the Hôtel de Russie), and duly executing then and there his will in favour of Colin Churchill as trustee, Audouin sauntered down gloomily to the San Paolo station, and took the train by himself to a miserable little stopping place in the midst of the dreary desolate Campagna. It was a baking day, even in the narrow shaded streets of Rome itself; but out on the shadeless scorched-up Agro Romano the sun was pouring down with tropical fierceness upon the flat levels, one vast stretch of silent slopes, with lonely hollows interspersed at intervals, where even the sheep and cattle seemed to pant and stagger under the breathless heat of the Italian noontide. Audouin got out at the wayside road, gave up his ticket to the dirty military-looking official, passed the osteria and the half dozen feverish yellow-washed houses that clustered round the obtrusive modern railway, and turned away from the direction of the mouldering village on the projecting buttress of rock towards the mysterious, melancholy, treeless desert on the other side. It was just the place for Audouin to walk alone on such a day, with his whole heart sick and weary of a generous attempt ill frustrated by the unaccountable caprice of fate. He had tried to do his best for Hiram Winthrop, and he had only succeeded in making himself and his friend supremely unhappy. Audouin had never cared much for life, and he cared less for it that day than ever before. 'After all,' he said to himself, 'what use is existence to me? I had one mistress, nature: I have almost tired of her: she palled upon me, and I wanted another. That other would not take my homage; and nature, it seems, in a fit of jealousy, has revenged her slighted pretensions upon me, in most unfeminine fashion, by making herself less beautiful in my eyes than formerly. How dull and gloomy it all looks to-day! What a difficult world to live in, what an easy world to leave; if we had but the trick to do it!'

He walked along quickly, away from the hills and the village perched on an outlying spur of the distant Apennines, on to the summit of a rolling undulation in that great grassy sea of wave-like hillocks. Not a sound stirred the stagnant air. Away in front, towards the dim distant Mediterranean, the flat prairies of Ostia steamed visibly in the flickering sunlight; a low region of reeds and cane-brake, with feathery herbage unruffled by any passing breath of wind, and barely relieved from utter monotony by the wide dry umbrella-shaped bosses of the basking stone-pines of Castel Fusano. The malaria seemed to hang over it like a terrible pall, blinking before the eye over the heated reach of sweltering pasture lands. Yonder lay Alsium—Palo they call it nowadays—a Dutch oven of pestilence, breeding miasma in its thousand foul nooks for the inoculation of all the country round. In truth a sickly, sickening spot; but here, Audouin whispered to himself half apologetically, with self-evident hypocrisy, here on the higher moorlands of the Campagna, among the shepherds and the sheep, beside the shaggy briar and hillocks, a man may walk and not hurt himself surely. Colin Churchill had said, 'No suicide;' and that was a bargain between them; yet suicide was one thing, and a quiet afternoon stroll through the heart of the country was really another.

He had bought a flask of 'sincere wine' at the osteria, and had brought some biscuits with him in his pocket from Rome. He meant to lunch out here on the Campagna, and only return late to the hotel for dinner. When a man feels broken and dispirited, what more natural than that he should wish to escape by himself for a lonely tramp in the fields and meadows, where none will interrupt his flow of spleen and the run of his solitary meditations?

It would be quite untrue to say that Lothrop Audouin had come into the Campagna by himself that day on purpose to catch the Roman fever. Nothing could be more unjust or unkind to him. Wayward natures like his do not expect to have their actions so harshly judged by the unsympathetic tribunal of common-sense. They seldom do anything on purpose. Audouin was only tempting nature. He was trusting to the chapter of accidents. A man has a right to walk over the ground (if unenclosed and unappropriated) whenever he chooses; there can be nothing wrong in taking a little turn by oneself even among the desolate surging undulations of the great plain that rolls illimitably between Rome and Civita Vecchia. He was exercising his undoubted rights as an American citizen; he could go where he chose over those long unfenced slopes, where you may walk in a straight line for miles ahead, with nothing to hinder you save the sun and the fever. And the fever! Well, yes; he did perhaps have some slight passing qualms of conscience on that head, when he thought of his promise to Colin Churchill; but then of course that was straining language—interpreting it in non-natural senses. A man isn't bound to make a mollycoddle of himself simply because he has promised a friend that he won't commit suicide.

He sat down in the eye of the sun on a bit of broken rock —or at least it looked like rock, though it was really a fragment from the concrete foundations of some ancient villa—with his legs dangling over the deep brown bank of pozzolano earth, and his hat slouched deeply above his eyes to protect him from the penetrating sunlight. Dead generations lay beneath his feet; the air was heavy with the dust of unnumbered myriads. Lothrop Audouin took out his flask and drank his wine and ate his biscuits. An old contadino came up suspiciously to watch the stranger; Audouin offered him the remainder of the wine, and the man drank it off at a gulp and thanked his excellency with Italian profuseness.

Would his excellency buy a coin, the contadino went on slowly, with the insinuating Roman begging whine. Audouin looked at the thing carelessly, and turned it round once or twice in his fingers. It was a denarius of Trajan, apparently; he could read the inscription, Avg. Ger. Dac. p.m. Tri. pot. Cos. vii., and so forth. It might be worth half a lire or so. He gave the man two lire for it. Suicide indeed! Who talks of suicide? Mayn't a bit of a virtuoso come out on to the Campagna, quite legitimately, to collect antiquities?

The fancy pleased him, and he talked awhile with the contadino about the things he had found in the galleries that honeycomb for miles the whole Campagna. Yes, the man had once found a beautiful scarabæus, a scarabæus that might have belonged to Cæsar or St. Peter. He had found a lachrymatory, too, a relic of an ancient Christian; and many bones of holy martyrs. How did he know they were holy martyrs? The most illustrious was joking. When one finds bones in a catacomb, one knows they must have been preserved by miraculous interference.

Much ague on the Campagna? No, no, signor; an air most salubrious, most vital, most innocent. In the Ptfntine Swamps? oh there, by Bacchus, excellency, it is far different. *There*, the people die of fever by hundreds; it is a most desolate country; encumbered with dead and rotting vegetation, it procreates miasma, and is left to stagnate idly in the sun. The bottoms are all soft slime and ooze, where buffaloes wallow and wild boars hide. Nothing there save a solitary pot-house, and a few quaking, quavering, ague-smitten contadini—a bad place to live in, the Pontine

Marshes, excellency. But here on the Agro Romano, high and dry, thanks to the Madonna and all holy saints, why, body of Bacchus, there is no malaria.

Or if any, very little. Towards nightfall, perhaps; yes, just a trifle towards nightfall; but what of that? One wraps one's sheepskin close around one; one takes care to be home early; one offers a candle now and then to the blessed Madonna; and the malaria is nothing. Except for foreigners. Ah, yes, foreigners ought always to be very sure not to stop out beyond nightfall.

Audouin let the man run on as long as he chose, and when the contadino was tired of conversation, he lay back upon the dry yellow grass, and thought bitterly to himself about life and fate, and Gwen and Hiram. What a miserable, foolish, impossible sort of world we all lived in after all! He had more money himself than he needed; he didn't want the nasty stuff—filthy lucre—filthy indeed in these days; dirty bank-notes, Italian or American, the first perhaps a trifle the dirtier and racrgeder of the two. He didn't want it, and Hiram for need of it was going to the wall; and yet he couldn't give it to Hiram, and Hiram wouldn't take it if he were to give it to him. Absurd conventionality! There was Gwen, too; Gwen; how happy he could make them both, if only they would let him; and yet, and yet, the thing was impossible. If only Hiram had those few wretched thousand dollars, scraps and scrips, shares and houses—Audouin didn't know exactly what they were or what was the worth of them; a lawyer in Boston managed the rubbish—if only Hiram had them, he could take to landscape, marry Gwen, and undo the evil that he, Lothrop Audouin, had unwittingly and unwillingly wrought in his foolish self-confidence, and live happily ever after. In fairy tales and novels and daydreams everybody always did live happy ever after—it's a way they have, somehow or other. The whole course of individual human history for the great Anglo-

American race, in fancy anyhow, seems always to end with a wedding as its natural finale and grand consummation. Yet here he was, boxed up alone with all that useless money, and the only way he could possibly do any good with it was by ceasing to exist altogether. No suicide! oh, no, certainly not. Still, if quite accidentally he happened to get the Roman fever, nobody would be one penny the worse for it, while Gwen and Hiram would doubtless be a good deal the better.

The afternoon wore away slowly, and evening came on at last across the great shifting desolate panorama. The dirty greens and yellows began to flush into gold and crimson; the misty haze from the Pontine Marshes began to creep with deadly stealth across the Agro Romano; the grey veil began to descend upon the softening Alban hills in the murky distance; the purples on the hillside hollows began to darken into gloomy shadows. A little breeze had sprung up meanwhile, and rain was dropping slowly from invisible light drifting clouds upon the parched Campagna. The malaria is never so dangerous as after a slight rain, that just damps the dusty surface without really penetrating it; for then the germs that lie thick among the mouldering vegetation are quickened into spasmodic life, and the whole Campagna steams and simmers with invisible eddies of vaporous effluvia. But Audouin sat there still, moodily pretending to himself that his headache would be all the better for a few cooling drops upon his feverish forehead. Even the old contadino was on his way back to his wretched hut, and as he passed he begged his excellency to get back to the railway with the most rapid expedition. 'Fa cattivo tempo,' he cried with a warning gesture. But his excellency only strolled slowly towards the yellow-washed station, dawdling by the way to watch the shadows as they grew deeper and blacker and ever longer on the distant indentations of the circling amphitheatre of hills.

The sunset glow faded away into ashen greyness. The air

struck cold and chill across the treeless levels. The wind swept harder and damper over the malarious lowland. Then the Campagna was swallowed up in dark, and Lothrop Audouin found his way alone, wet and steaming, to the tiny roadside station. The train from Civita Vecchia was not due for half an hour yet; he stood on the platform under the light wooden covering, and waited for it to come in with a certain profound internal sense of despairing resignation. His limbs were very cold, and his forehead was absolutely burning. Yes, yes, thank heaven for that! the chapter of accidents had not forsaken him. He felt sure he had caught the Roman fever.

When the English doctor came to see him at the hotel that evening, about eleven, the work of diagnosis was short and easy. 'Country fever in its worst and most dangerous form,' he said simply; 'in fact what we at Rome are accustomed to call the *perniciosa*.'

CHAPTER XLV. HOVERING.

Acute Roman fever is a very serious matter. For seven days Audouin lay in extreme danger, hovering between life and death, with the crisis always approaching but never actually arriving. Every day, when the English doctor came to see him, Audouin asked feebly from his pillow, 'Am I getting worse?' and the doctor, who fancied he was a nervous man, answered cheerfully, 'Well, no, not worse; about the same again this morning, though I'm afraid I can't exactly say you're any better. Audouin turned round wearily with a sigh, and thought to himself, 'How hard a thing it is to die, after all, even when you really want to.'

Colin Churchill came to see him as soon as ever he heard of his illness, and sitting in the easy-chair by the sick man's bedside, he said to him in a reproachful tone, 'Mr. Audouin, you don't play fair. You've broken the spirit of the agreement. Our compact was, no suicide. Now, I'm sure you've been recklessly exposing yourself out upon the Campagna, or else why should you have got this fever so very suddenly?'

Audouin smiled a faint smile from the bed, and answered half incoherently, 'Chapter of accidents. Put your trust in bad luck, and verily you will not be disappointed. But I'm afraid it's a terribly long and tedious piece of work, this dying.'

'If you weren't so ill,' Colin answered gravely and sternly, 'I think I should have to be very angry with you. You haven't stood by the spirit of the contract. As it is, we must do our best to defeat your endeavours, and bring you back to life again.'

Audouin moved restlessly in the bed. 'You must do your

146

worst, I recognise,' he said; 'but I don't think you'll get the better of the fever for all that: she's a goddess, you know, and had her temple once upon the brow of the Palatine. Many have prayed to her to avoid them; it must be a novelty for her to hear a prayer for her good company. Perhaps she may be merciful to her only willing votary. But she's long about it; she might have got through by this time. Anyhow, you mustn't be too hard upon me, Churchill.'

As for Hiram, Audouin's illness came upon him like a final thunderclap. Everything had gone ill with him lately; he had reached almost the blackest abyss of despondency already; and if Audouin were to die now, he felt that his cup of bitterness would be overflowing. Besides, though he knew nothing, of course, of Audouin's interview with Colin Churchill, he had a grave suspicion in his own mind that his friend had egged himself into an illness by brooding over Truman's visit and Hiram's own proposals for returning to America. Of course all that was laid aside now, at least for the present. Whatever came, he must stop and nurse Audouin; and he nursed him with all the tender care and delicacy of a woman.

Gwen came round often, too, and sat watching in the sick-room for hours together. The colonel objected to it seriously—so very extraordinary, you know; indeed, really quite compromising; but Gwen was not to be kept away by the colonel's scruples and prejudices; so she watched and waited in her own good time, taking turns with Hiram in day and night nursing. It was all perfect misery to Audouin; the more he wanted to die for Gwen's and Hiram's convenience, the more utterly determined they both seemed to be to keep him living somehow at all hazards.

On the seventh day, the crisis came, and Audouin began to sink rapidly. Gwen and Hiram were both by his bedside, and Colin Churchill and Minna were waiting anxiously in the little salon alongside. When the doctor came, he stopped longer than usual; and as he passed out, Colin asked him what news this morning of the poor patient. The doctor twirled his watch-chain quietly. 'Well,' he said, in his calm professional manner, 'I should say it was probable he would get through the night; but I doubt if he'll live over Sunday.'

'Then there's no hope, you think?' Minna asked with tears in her eyes.

'Well, I couldn't exactly say that,' the doctor answered. 'A medical man always hopes to the last moment, especially in acute diseases. The critical point's hardly reached yet. Oh yes, he might recover; he might recover, certainly; but it isn't likely.'

Colin and Minna sat down once more in the empty salon, and looked at one another long, without speaking. At last there came a knock at the door. Colin answered 'Enter,' and a servant entered. 'A card for Signor Vintrop,' he said, handing it to Colin. 'The bringer says he must see him on important business immediately.'

Colin cast a careless glance at the card. It was that of a well-known Roman picture-dealer, agent for one of the largest firms of fine art auctioneers in London. 'How very ill-timed,' he said to Minna, handing her the card. At any other moment, Hiram would have been delighted; but it's quite impossible to trouble him with this at such a crisis.

'Does he want to buy some of Mr. Winthrop's pictures, do you think, Colin?' Minna asked anxiously.

'I'm sure he does; but it can't be helped now. Tell the gentleman that Mr. Winthrop can't see him now, if you please, Antonio. He's watching by the side of the American signor who is dying.'

Antonio bowed and went out. In a minute he returned once more. 'The person can't wait,' he said; 'the affair is

148

urgent. He wishes to give Signor Vintrop an important commission. He wishes to buy pictures, many pictures, immediately. He has come from the studio, hearing that Signor Vintrop was at the hotel, and he wishes particularly to speak with him instantaneously.'

Colin looked at Minna and shook his head.

'This is very annoying, really, Minna,' he said with a sigh. 'At any other time, it would have been a perfect godsend; but now—one can't drag him away from poor Audouin's bedside. Tell the gentleman, Antonio,' he went on in Italian, 'that Mr. Winthrop can't possibly see him. It is most absolutely and decidedly impossible.'

Antonio went away, and for half an hour more Colin and Minna conversed together in an undertone without further interruption. Then a knock came again, and Antonio entered with a second card. It bore the name of another famous Roman picture-dealer, the agent for the rival London firm. 'He says he must see Signor Vintrop without delay,' Antonio reported, 'upon important business of the strictest urgency.'

Colin hesitated a moment. 'This is really very remarkable, Minna,' he said slowly, turning over the card in great perplexity. 'Why on earth should the two principal picture-dealers in Rome want to see Hiram Winthrop so very particularly on the same morning?'

'I can't imagine,' Minna answered, looking at the card curiously. 'Don't you think, Colin, you'd better see the man and ask him what's the meaning of it?'

Colin nodded assent, and went to the door to speak to the dealer. As he did so, a second servant stepped up with yet another card, that of a Manchester picture-agent in person.

'What do you want to see Mr. Winthrop for in such a hurry?' Colin asked the Italian dealer. 'How is it you all wish to buy his pictures the same morning? He's been in

Rome a good many years now, but nobody ever seemed in any great haste to become a purchaser.'

'I cannot tell you, signor,' the dealer answered blandly; 'but I have my instructions from London. I have a telegram direct from a most illustrious firm, requesting me to buy up the landscapes, and especially the American landscapes, of Signor Vintrop.'

'And if Mr. Winthrop's too ill himself to come and show me his studio,' the Manchester agent put in, in English, 'perhaps, sir, you might step round yourself and arrange matters with me on his behalf.'

Colin hesitated a moment. It was an awkward predicament. He didn't like to go away selling pictures when Audouin was actually dying; and yet, knowing what he knew, and taking into consideration Audouin's particular mental constitution, he saw in it a possible chance of saving his life indirectly. Something or other had occurred, that was clear, to make a sudden demand arise for Hiram's pictures. If the demand was a genuine one, and if he could sell them for good prices, the effect upon Audouin might be truly magical. The man was really dying, not of fever, of that Colin felt certain, but of hopeless chagrin and disappointment. If he could only learn that Hiram's landscapes were meeting with due appreciation after all, he might perhaps even now recover.

Colin went back to Minna for a few minutes' whispered conversation; and then, having learned from Gwen (without telling her his plans) that Audouin was no worse, and that he would probably go on without serious change for some hours, he hurried off to the studio between the two intending purchasers.

As he got to the door, he saw a small crowd of artistic folk, mostly agents or dealers, and amongst them he noticed a friend and fellow-student at Maragliano's, the young

Englishman, Arthur Forton. 'Why, what on earth's the meaning of this, Forton?' he asked in fresh amazement. 'All the world seems to have taken suddenly to besieging Winthrop's studio.'

'Ah, yes,' Forton answered briskly; 'I thought there was sure to be a run upon his bank after what I saw in Truman's paper; and I happened to be at Raffaele Pedrocchi's when a telegram came in from Magnus of London asking him to buy up all Winthrop's landscapes that he could lay his hands upon at once, and especially authorising him to pay up to something in cypher for Chattawauga Lake or some such heathenish Yankee name or other. So I came round immediately to see Winthrop, and advise him not to let the things go for a mere song, as Magnus is evidently anxious to get them almost at any price.'

Colin listened in profound astonishment. 'Truman's paper!' he cried in surprise. 'Why, Winthrop positively assured me that Truman told him he ought to go back at once to America.'

'So he did, no doubt,' Forton replied carelessly. 'Indeed, he tells him so in print in *Fortuna Melliflua*. Here's the cutting: I cut it out on purpose, so that Winthrop might take care he wasn't chiselled, as you were, you know, over "Autumn and the Breezes."'

Colin took the scrap of paper from the little pamphlet from Forton's hands, and read the whole paragraph through with a thrill of pleasure.

'And yet from this same entirely damned land of America,' ran Mr. Truman's candid and vigorous criticism, 'some good thing may haply come, even as (cynical Nathaniel to the contrary notwithstanding) some good thing did indubitably come out of Nazareth of Galilee. The other day, walking by chance into a certain small shabby studio, down a side alley from the Street of the Beautiful Ladies at Rome, I

151

unearthed there busily at work upon a Babylonian Woe one Hiram Winthrop, an American artist, who had fled from America and the City of Destruction to come enthusiastically Romeward. He had better far have stopped at home. For this young man Winthrop, a God-sent landscape painter, if ever there was one, has in truth the veritable eye for seeing and painting a bit of overgrown rank waterside vegetation exactly as nature herself originally disposed it, with no nice orthodox and academical graces of arrangement, but simply so—weeds and water—no more than that; just a tangled corner of neglected reeds and waving irises, seen in an aerial perspective which is almost stereoscopic. Strange to say, this American savage from the wild woods can reproduce the wild woods from which he came, in all their native wildness, without the remotest desire to make them look like a Dutch picture of the garden of Eden. Moreover, he positively knows that red things are red, green things green, and white things white; a piece of knowledge truly remarkable in this artificially colour-blind age of dichroic vision (I get my fine words from a scientific treatise on the subject by Professor Stilling of Leipzig, to whose soul may heaven be merciful). There was one picture of his there—Chattawauga Lake I think he called it—which I had it in my mind to buy at the moment, and had even gone so far as to purse up my lips into due form for saying, "How much is it?" (as we price spring chickens at market), but on deeper thought, I refrained deliberately, because I am now a poor man, and I do not want to buy pictures at low rates, being fully of opinion, on good warranty, that the labourer is worthy of his hire. So I left it, more out of political than personal economy, for some wealthier man to buy hereafter. Yet whoever does buy Chattawauga Lake (the name alone is too repellant) will find himself in possession, I do not hesitate to say, of the finest bit of entirely sincere and scrupulous landscape that has ever been painted since

152

Turner's brush lay finally still upon his broken palette. And young Mr. Hiram Wintlirop himself, I dare predict, will go back to America hereafter and give us other landscapes which will more than suffice to wash out the Babylonian woes whereupon he is at present engaged in sedulously wasting a most decisive and categorical genius.'

Colin took the scrap of paper in his hands, and went with Forton into the disorderly studio.

'May I take it to show Winthrop and Audouin?' he asked.

Forton nodded.

They turned to the pictures, and Chattawauga Lake having been duly produced, Colin found himself at a moment's notice turned into a sort of amateur auctioneer, receiving informal bids one after another from the representatives of almost all the best picture firms in the whole of England.

He had soon got rid of Chattawauga Lake, and before an hour and a half was over, the agents had almost made a clean sweep of the entire studio. Even the Babylonian Woe was bought up at a fair price by one enthusiastic person, on the ground that it had been immensely enhanced in value by being mentioned, although unfavourably, in a note of Truman's. The great critic had simply made Hiram Winthrop's fortune; people were prepared to buy anything he might paint now, on the strength of Truman's recommendation.

As soon as Colin had got rid of the more pressing purchasers, he left Forton in charge of the studio, and ran back hastily to Audouin's hotel. Would the good news be in time to save the dying man's life? that was the question. Colin wondered what he could make of it, and turned over the matter anxiously in his own mind, as he went back to Minna, Gwen, and Hiram.

CHAPTER XLVI. AUDOUIN SINKS OR SWIMS.

C olin entered the little salon once more with bated breath and eager anxiety. 'Is he alive yet, Minna?' he asked in a low tone, as she came to meet him, pale and timid.

'Alive, Colin, but hardly more. The fever's very serious, and Miss Russell says he's wandering in his mind terribly.'

'What's he saying, Minna? Did Miss Russell tell you?'

'Oh, yes, poor girl; she's crying her eyes out. She says, Colin, he's muttering that he has ruined Mr. Winthrop, and that he wished he was dead, and then they'd both be happy.' Colin went in without another word to the sick-room, and stood awhile by the bedside, listening anxiously to poor Audouin's incoherent mutterings. As he caught a word or two of his troubled thoughts, he made up his mind at once as to what he must do. Taking Hiram by the arm, he drew him quietly without a word into the salon. 'Winthrop,' he said, 'I have something to explain to you. You must listen to it now, though it sounds irrelevant, because it's really a matter of life and death to Mr. Audouin. I've just sold your Chattawauga Lake for seven thousand five hundred lire.

Hiram started in surprise for a moment, and then made a gesture of impatience. 'What does that matter, my dear fellow,' he cried, 'when Mr. Audouin's just dying?'

'It matters a great deal,' Colin answered; 'and if you'll wait and hear, you'll see it may be the means of saving his life for you.'

Hiram sat down and listened with blanched face to Colin's story. Then Colin began at the beginning and told him all he knew: how Audouin had lost heart entirely at

155

Hiram's want of success; how he had made a will, practically in Hiram's favour; and how he had gone out quite deliberately upon the Campagna, and caught the *perniciosa*, on purpose to kill himself for Hiram's benefit. At this point Hiram interrupted him for a moment. His lips were deadly pale, and he trembled violently, but he said in his usual calm voice, 'You do him an injustice there, Churchill. He didn't do it on purpose. I know him better than you do. Whatever he did, he did half unconsciously by way of meeting fate half way only. Mr. Audouin is quite incapable of breaking his promise.'

Colin heard him and nodded acquiescence. It was no time, indeed, for discussing the abstract points of Audouin's character. Then he went on with his story, telling Hiram how the picture-dealers had come to him that morning, how he had sold Chattawauga Lake and several other of his pieces for excellent prices, and how the influx had been wholly due to a single paragraph in Truman's 'For-tuna Melliflua.' As he spoke he handed Hiram the cutting to read, and Hiram read it rapidly through with an unwonted sense of relief and freedom 'I don't know, Churchill,' he said when he had finished. 'I can't feel sure of it. But I think it has come in time to save his life for us.'

They concerted a little scheme shortly between them, and then they went into the sick-room once more, where Audouin was now lying somewhat more quietly with his eyes half open. Hiram held up his head and gave him a dose of the mixture which had been ordered for him at moments of feebleness. It seemed to revive him a little. Then they sat down by the bed together, and began talking to one another in a low tone, so that Audouin could easily overhear them. He was less feverish, for the moment, and seemed quite sensible; so Colin said in a quiet voice, 'Yes, I sold Chattawauga Lake to old Focacci, who acts as agent, you

156

know, for Magnus of London.'

Audouin evidently overheard the words, and took in their meaning vaguely, for his eye turned towards Colin, and he seemed to listen with some attention.

'How much did you sell it for?' asked Hiram. He hated himself for even seeming to be thus talking about his own wretched pecuniary business when Audouin was perhaps dying, but he knew it was the only chance of rousing his best and earliest friend from that fatal torpor.

'Seven thousand five hundred lire,' answered Colin.

'How much is that in our money?'

'In English money, three hundred pounds sterling,' Colin replied, distinctly.

There was a little rustling in the bed, an attempt to sit up feebly, and then Audouin asked in a parched voice, 'How many dollars?' 'Hush, hush, Mr. Audouin,' Colin said gently, pretending to check him, but feeling in his own heart that their little ruse had almost succeeded already. 'You mustn't excite yourself on any account.'

Audouin was silent for a moment; then he said again, in a somewhat stronger and more decided manner, 'How many dollars, I say: how many dollars?'

'Five into seven thousand five hundred' Hiram reckoned with a slight shudder, 'makes fifteen hundred, doesn't it, Churchill? Yes, fifteen hundred. Fifteen hundred dollars, Mr. Audouin.'

Audouin fell back upon the pillow, for he had raised his head slightly once more, and seemed for a while to be dozing quietly. At lust he asked again, 'Who to, did you say?'

'Focacci of the Piazza di Spagna, agent for Magnus and Hickson of London.'

This time, Audouin lay a long while ruminating in his

fevered head over that last important disclosure. He seemed to take it in faintly bit by bit, for after another long pause he asked even more deliberately, 'How did Magnus and Rickson ever come to hear of you, Hiram?'

Colin thought the time had now come to tell him briefly the good news in its entirety, if it was to keep him from dying of disappointment. 'Truman has written very favourably about Winthrop's abilities as a landscape painter,' he said gently, 'in his "Fortuna Melliflua," and a great many London dealers have sent telegrams to buy up all his pictures. I have been round to the studio this morning, and sold almost all of them at high prices.

Truman has spoken so well of them that there can be very little doubt Winthrop's fortune is fairly made in real earnest.'

They watched Audouin carefully as Colin spoke, for they feared the excitement might perhaps have been too much for him: it was a risky card to play, but they played it in all good intention. Audouin listened quite intelligently to the end, and then he suddenly burst out crying. For some minutes he cried silently, without even a sob to break the deathlike stillness. The tears seemed to do him good, too; for as he cried, Gwen, hanging over him eagerly, noticed that little beads of moisture were beginning to form faintly upon his parched forehead. In their concentrated anxiety for Audouin's life, neither she nor Hiram had yet found time adequately to realise their own good fortune; they could only think of its effect upon the crisis of that terrible fever.

Audouin cried on without a word for ten minutes, and then he asked once more, in a weak voice, 'What did Truman say? Have you got "Fortuna?"'

Colin took out the paragraph once more and read it all over, omitting only the Babylonian Woe, which he feared might have the effect of distressing Audouin. When he had finished, Audouin smiled, and answered, smiling faintly, with a touch of his wonted self, 'Then, like Wolfe, I shall die happy;' and after a moment he added, in a feebly theatrical fashion, 'They run. Who run? The Philistines, to buy his pictures. Then I die happy.'

'No, no, Mr. Audouin,' Gwen cried passionately, lifting his white hand to her lips and kissing it fervidly. 'You mustn't die. For our sakes, you must try to live and share all our happiness.'

Audouin shook his head slowly. 'No, no,' he said; 'the fever has got too strong a hold upon me. I shall never, never recover.'

'You must, Mr. Audouin,' Colin Churchill said resolutely. 'If you go and die after all, I shall never forgive you. You've got nothing to die for now, and you mustn't think of going at last and doing anything so wicked and foolish.'

Audouin smiled again, and turning over on his side, began to doze off in a feverish sleep. He slept so long and so soundly that Gwen was frightened, and insisted upon sending for the doctor. When the doctor came, it was growing dark, and Audouin lay still and peaceful like a child in the cradle. The doctor felt his pulse without awakening him. 'Why,' he cried in surprise, 'he seems to have been very much excited, but his pulse is decidedly fuller and slower than it was this morning. Something unexpected must have occurred to make an improvement in his condition. I think the crisis is over, and he'll get round again in time with good nursing.' Gwen and the hired nurse sat up all that night with him.

CHAPTER XLVII. ALL'S WELL THAT ENDS WELL.

Audouin's recovery was slow, of course; but, he did recover; and as soon as he was safely out of all danger, Gwen and Hiram, now fairly on the road to fortune, proposed that they should forthwith marry. The colonel had almost given up active opposition by this time; he knew that that girl's temper was absolutely ungovernable; and besides, they said the shock-headed Yankee fellow was beginning to make quite a decent livelihood out of his painting business. So the colonel merely answered when Gwen mentioned to him the date she had fixed upon, 'You'll go your own way, I suppose, Miss, whatever I choose to say to you about it,' and threw no further obstacles in the way of the ceremony.

'And, Gwen,' Hiram said to her, as they walked together down the path by the Casca-telli at Tivoli a few days before the wedding, 'we'll take the Tyrol, if you'd like it, for our wedding tour, darling.'

'Yes,' Gwen answered, 'we will, and we'll never come back again to Rome, to live I mean, Hiram, but go to Switzerland, or Wales, or Scotland, or America. You must go, you know, where you can find what you most want to paint—your own beautiful delicate landscapes. I always knew that that was what you could do best; and I always told you that there at least you had real genius.' Hiram's answer was of a sort that cannot readily be put down in definite language; and yet Gwen understood it perfectly, and only murmured in a low soft tone, 'Not here, Hiram, not here, there's a dear good fellow.'

The bushes around were fairly thick and screening, to be

161

sure, but still, in the open air, you know, and in a place overrun with tourists, like Tivoli—well, it was certainly very imprudent.

When Colin Churchill heard that Hiram and Gwen had definitely fixed the day for their own wedding, he put on his hat and went round to the English quarter to call for Minna. They walked together up from the Piazza del Popolo, by the Pincian and Esquiline, towards the straggling vineyards on the Colian Hill. There the young vines were coming into the first fresh leaf, and the air was thick with perfume from the jonquils and lilacs in the neighbouring flower gardens.

'Minna darling,' Colin began quietly, and Minna flushed crimson and thrilled through to her inmost marrow at the sound of the words, for Colin had never before called her 'darling.' She looked at him full of tender surmise, and her bursting heart stood still for a moment within her bosom, waiting to know whether it was to bound again with joy, or flutter feebly in disappointment. After all, then, Colin Churchill really loved her!

Colin noticed the evident tokens of suspense upon her dark cheek, with the hot blood struggling red through the rich gipsy complexion, and wondered to himself that she should feel so deeply moved by the simple question he was going to ask her. Had they not always loved one another, all their lives long, and was it not a mere question of time and convenience, now, the particular day they fixed upon for their marriage? He could hardly understand the profoundness of her emotion, though he was too practised an observer of the human face not to read it readily in her flushed features: for, after all, it was nothing more than settling the final arrangements for a foregone conclusion.

'Minna darling,' he said once more, watching her narrowly all the time, 'Win-throp and Miss Howard-Russell are going to be married on Thursday fortnight. I was thinking, dearest, that if you could arrange it with your people so soon, it'd be a good plan for us to have our wedding at the same time, for I suppose you don't think a fortnight too short notice after such a long engagement?'

Minna trembled violently from head to foot as she answered, with a little tremor in her voice, 'Then Colin, Colin, oh Colin, you really love me!'

Colin caught her small round hand tenderly in his and said, with a tone of genuine surprise, 'Why, you know perfectly well, my own darling little Minna, I've always loved you dearly. All my life long, darling, I've always loved you.'

It was well that Colin held the round brown hand tight in his, that moment, for as Minna heard those words— those words that her heart had longed so long to hear, and whose truth she had doubted to herself so often—she uttered a little loud sharp cry, and fell forward, not fainting, but overcome with too sudden joy, so that her head reeled, and she might have dropped unconscious, but that Colin caught her, and pressed her in his arms, and kissed lier, and cried to her in surprise and self-reproach, 'Why, Minna, Minna, darling Minna, my own heart's darling, you knew I loved you; you must have known I always loved you.'

Minna's heart fluttered up and down within her bosom, and heaved and swelled as though it would burst asunder that tight little plain black bodice. (Why do not dressmakers allow something for the natural expansiveness of emotion, I wonder.) It was so sweet to hear Colin say so; and yet even now she could hardly believe her life-long daydream had wrought out at last its own fulfillment. 'Oh, Colin, Colin,' she murmured through her tears—for she had found that relief—'you never told me so; you never, never told me you loved me.'

163

'Told you, Minna!' Colin cried with another kiss upon the trembling lips (and all this on the open Colian too); 'told you, Minna darling! Why, who on earth would ever have dreamt of deliberately telling you. But you must have known it; of course you must have known it. Haven't we been lovers together, darling, from our babyhood upward?'

'But that was just it, Colin,' Minna answered, brushing away her tears, and trying to look as if nothing extraordinary at all had happened. 'We had always known one another, of course, and been very fond of one another, like old companions, and I wasn't sure, with you, Colin, whether it was love or merely friendship.'

'And with yourself, Minna?' Cohn asked, taking her soft wee hand once more between his own two; 'tell me, darling, which was it, which was it?'

Minna's face gave her only answer, and Colin accepted it silently with another kiss.

There was a minute's pause again (the Colian is really such a very awkward place for lovemaking, with all those horrid prying old priests poking about everywhere), and then Minna began once more: 'You see, Colin, you seemed so cold and indifferent. You were always so wrapped up in your marble and your statues, and you didn't appear to care a bit for anything but art, till I almost grew to hate it. Oh, Colin, I know the things you make are the most beautiful that ever were moulded, but I almost hated them, because you seemed to think of nothing on earth but your clay and your sculpture. I was afraid you only liked me; I didn't feel sure whether you really loved me.'

'Minna,' Colin said soberly, standing up before her and looking full into those bright black eyes straight in front of him, 'I love you with all the love in my nature. I have loved you ever since we were children together, and I have never for one moment ceased from loving you. How could I, when

164

you were Minna? If I ever seemed cold and careless, darling, it was only because I loved you so thoroughly and unquestioningly that it didn't occur to me to waste words in telling you what I thought you yourself could never question. My darling, if I've caused you doubt or pain, I can't tell you how sorry I am for it. I have worked for you, and for you only, all these years. Don't you remember, little woman, long ago at Wootton, how I always used to make images for Minna?

Well, I've been making images for Minna ever since. I never for a moment fancied you didn't know it. But now, as I love you, and as you love me, tell me, darling, will you marry me on Thursday fortnight? Don't say no, or wait to think about it, but answer me "yes" at once; now do'ee, Minna, do'ee.'

That half-unconscious, half-artful return on Colin's part to the old loved familiar dialect of their peasant childhood was more than Minna's bursting little heart could ever have resisted, even if she had wanted to—which she certainly didn't. With the tears once more trickling slowly down her cheek, she answered softly, 'Yes, Colin;' and Colin pressed her hand a second time in token of the completed contract. And then the two turned slowly back towards the great city, and Minna tried to dry her eyes and look as though nothing at all out of the way had happened against her return to the Via Clementina.

'Bits that exactly suit Hiram's canvas.'

Original

Gwen and Hiram Winthrop, in their little cottage in North Wales, are within easy reach of many wild bits that exactly suit Hiram's canvas. His natural genius has full play now, and at the Academy every year there are few pictures more studiously avoided by the crowd, and more carefully observed by the best judges, than Mr. Winthrop's, the famous American landscape painter's. Now and then he pays a short visit to America, and sketches unbroken nature, as he alone can sketch it, in the Adirondacks, and the White Mountains, and the Upper Alleghanies; but for the most part, as Gwen simply phrases it, 'Wales and Scotland are quite good enough for us.' Once a year, too, he runs across for a month or six weeks to Rome and Florence, where Colin and Minna are always glad to give him and his wife a hearty welcome. Even the colonel has relented somewhat in a grim official Anglo-Indian fashion, and as he jogs Gwen's youngest boy upon his knee to the tune of some Hindustani jingle about Warren Hastings, he reflects to himself that after all that shockheaded Yankee painter fellow isn't really such a bad sort of person by way of a son-in-law.

And Audouin? Audouin has sold Lakeside, and flits to and fro uneasily between Europe and America in a somewhat vague and purposeless fashion. Sometimes he stops with Colin Churchill at Rome (on a strict pledge that he won't go out alone without leave to stroll upon the Campagna), and sometimes he wanders by himself, knapsack on back, among the Swiss or Tyrolese mountains; but most often he gravitates towards Bryn-y-mynydd, on the slopes of Aran, where Gwen still greets him always in most daughterly fashion with a kiss of welcome. Gwen's little boys are firm as a rock upon one point, that except daddy, there isn't a man in the world at all to be compared for starting a squirrel or scaring a pine marten to Uncle Audouin. But what his precise claim to uncleship may be is a genealogical question that has never for a moment troubled their simple unsophisticated little intellects. They hold ingenuously that a rocking-horse apiece upon their birthdays, and a bright new gold half-sovereign on every visit, is quite sufficient guarantee for that naïf and expansive title of kinship.

THE END.